❀ FOLK AND FAIRY TALES ❀

FOLK & FAIRY TALES

CONCISE EDITION

EDITED BY

MARTIN HALLETT & BARBARA KARASEK

broadview press

Library and Archives Canada Cataloguing in Publication

Folk & fairy tales / edited by Martin Hallett & Barbara Karasek. — Concise ed.

ISBN 978-1-55481-018-5

1. Fairy tales. 2. Tales. 3. Folk literature—History and criticism.
I. Hallett, Martin, 1944- II. Karasek, Barbara, 1954- III. Title: Folk and fairy tales.

PZ8.F65 2011   398.2   C2011-900543-3

Broadview Press is an independent, international publishing house, incorporated in 1985.

We welcome comments and suggestions regarding any aspect of our publications—please feel free to contact us at the addresses below or at broadview@broadviewpress.com.

North America
PO Box 1243, Peterborough, Ontario, Canada K9J 7H5
2215 Kenmore Ave., Buffalo, New York, USA 14207
Tel: (705) 743-8990; Fax: (705) 743-8353
email: customerservice@broadviewpress.com

UK, Europe, Central Asia, Middle East, Africa, India, and Southeast Asia
Eurospan Group, 3 Henrietta St., London WC2E 8LU, United Kingdom
Tel: 44 (0) 1767 604972; Fax: 44 (0) 1767 601640
email: eurospan@turpin-distribution.com

Australia and New Zealand
NewSouth Books
c/o TL Distribution, 15-23 Helles Ave., Moorebank, NSW, Australia 2170
Tel: (02) 8778 9999; Fax: (02) 8778 9944
email: orders@tldistribution.com.au

www.broadviewpress.com

Copy-edited by Betsy Struthers
Broadview Press acknowledges the financial support of the Government of Canada through the Canada Book Fund for our publishing activities.

The interior of this book is printed on paper containing 100% post-consumer fibre.

Design and composition by George Kirkpatrick
PRINTED IN CANADA

CONTENTS

PREFACE

THE PRIMARY PURPOSE OF THIS text is to provide the student with the opportunity to examine and compare a selection of classic fairy tales as part of a broader
study, whether it be in children's literature or cultural studies. Its parent, *Folk & Fairy
Tales*, currently in its fourth edition, offers a relatively comprehensive introduction
to the fairy tale and therefore runs to over four hundred pages. Those wishing to take
a shorter excursion through the world of fairy tales may find the present text more
suitable, in that it limits itself to exploring a small group of tales that might be termed
the *supernovas* of the fairy-tale firmament.

In preparing this new edition, we have been careful to remind ourselves that
this book is, first and foremost, an *introduction*. From the very beginning, we have
seen the typical reader of *Folk and Fairy Tales* as a student returning—somewhat
sceptically—to the fairy tale for the first time since elementary school or kindergar-
ten—or perhaps even professing to remember nothing about fairy tales that wasn't
derived from a Disney movie. At the same time, the valuable and much appreciated
feedback that we have received from those who have used *Folk and Fairy Tales* in
the classroom has helped us greatly in adjusting both our selection of tales and the
manner in which we present them, both to introduce some lesser-known versions of
famous tales and to encourage comparison between versions of one tale, or catego-
ries of several.

While the increasing multiculturalism of our society has brought with it many
riches, it nevertheless presents a problem for the teacher who must endeavor to find
some common ground for students from diverse cultural, social, and intellectual
backgrounds. In this context, the fairy tale offers a unique opportunity to introduce
students to a literary form that is familiar and simple, yet multidimensional. No
student can claim to be wholly ignorant of fairy tales, but it is highly unlikely that
he or she has ever gone beyond their surface simplicity to discover the surprisingly
subtle complexities that lie beneath.

Because the pedagogical technique of challenging expectations has been a major principle influencing our choice and juxtaposition of tales, most of those selected will quickly be recognized as "classics." It must be pointed out, however, that despite their popularity, these well-known tales are not representative of the international body of fairy tales. Since in this concise format we can only provide a modest selection of tales, it was our feeling that the greatest advantage could be achieved by guiding students through familiar territory while introducing some new perspectives. It will be the students' task, then, to apply these and other critical approaches more widely, not only to other fairy tales, but also to the whole world of literature.

We hope that the critical section, though brief, will illuminate some of the current issues that surround the fairy tale in contemporary times; in addition, the accompanying website will provide access to some additional material that could not be included in this new edition: <http://www.broadviewpress.com/tales/index .htm>.

INTRODUCTION

FAIRY TALE IS A TERM that is often used rather loosely. A dictionary will probably tell us that it is a story about fairies (which is often not the case), or else that it is an unbelievable or untrue story (which reflects the rationalistic criticism to which the fairy tale has been subjected). This vagueness of definition has made the term something of a catch-all: Lewis Carroll, for instance, described *Through the Looking-Glass* as a fairy tale, and Andrew Lang saw fit to include an abridged version of Book 1 of Swift's *Gulliver's Travels* in his *Blue Fairy Book*. So let us clarify the subject a little by introducing two more specific terms: "folk tale" and "literary tale." Once we have established the essential difference between these two terms, we will be in a better position to recognize the many permutations that have evolved over the years.

"Folk tale" means exactly what it says: it's a tale of the folk. If we resort again to our dictionary, we will learn that "folk" signifies the common people of a nation—and the important point to realize here is that the "common people" were, in the past, generally illiterate. Consequently, their tales were orally transmitted; in other words, they were passed down from generation to generation by word of mouth, until they were eventually recorded and published by such famous individuals as Charles Perrault and Jacob and Wilhelm Grimm. Because we hear so often of "Perrault's Fairy Tales" or of "Grimms' Fairy Tales," it's natural to assume that these men actually made them up, but that isn't the case; while all three were highly accomplished literary men, none of them were fairy-tale writers. They wrote them *down*, thereby creating what we may term a literary folk tale.

Consider for a moment what happens when a tale is transposed from oral performance. Even if the collectors of earlier times had had modern recording devices at their disposal, they still could not have published the tales exactly as they had heard them, for the simple reason that the spoken language is very different from the written. The judicious collector therefore had (and has) the task of making the tale "read" properly, which naturally involves the exercise of personal judgment and taste, thus imposing the "imprint" of this new intermediary. Moreover, the number of separate recorded versions of a single folk-tale type is sometimes quite amazing, reaching well into the hundreds. They come from all over the world, which presents us with some clues, and also some conundrums, about the universal use of story to help people come to terms with the fears, the challenges, and the mysteries that are all part of life.

In most cases, we have no idea how old folk tales are. Once a tale has been told, it is gone; no trace of it remains except in the memories of the teller and the audience. And for the great majority of people today, memory is a fickle instrument—we only have to think back to that examination, or to the last time we lost the shopping-list, to realize how quickly (and how thoroughly) we forget. We are thus confronted with the realization that the only authentic version of the folk tale is an oral version—and since one telling will necessarily differ from the next, we must confer authenticity equally on all tellings, or—even more problematic—on the first telling alone, wherever and whenever that may have taken place.

The children's party game "Broken Telephone" provides us with an idea of just how a folk tale may have evolved as it was passed on from generation to generation. The first player begins by whispering a phrase or sentence to his or her neighbor, who must then pass it on to the next, and so on until it reaches the last individual in the chain. Needless to say, in its progress from first to last, the words undergo some startling and often amusing changes, as they are variously misheard, misunderstood, or improved upon. On the simplest level, the game entertains by allowing us to play around with language and intention; on a more sophisticated level, we might see those changes as reflecting the preoccupations (conscious or otherwise) of the players. To put it another way, our moods, desires, and emotions will inevitably affect what is heard; we hear what we want (or expect) to hear. So it is with the folk tale; what we find there is—in part—a fragment of psychic history. An archaeologist unearths a piece of pottery and uses his professional experience and knowledge to determine its significance and function in the wider context. In the same way, we can use our growing familiarity with folk tales to identify some of the psychological elements (the "preoccupations") that give each tale much of its energy and color.

The archaeologist's discoveries generally end up in a museum—and that, in a sense, is what happens to the folk tale as well. Why use a word like "museum"? Because a museum is a place where you store and exhibit interesting dead things—and that is exactly what a folk tale is, once it's between the covers of a book. Even though a tale's oral existence may of course continue (there are even instances of literary tales becoming part of the oral tradition), the gradual spread of literacy has turned the oral tale into an endangered species; once the tale has been "frozen" in print, it can no longer evolve with telling and retelling, since one reading will be exactly the same as any other.

[10]

It would be an exaggeration, however, to claim that the oral tale is entirely a thing of the past. Although the urban legend is much more localized and anecdotal than the folk tale and is characterized by sensationalism and black humor, it too has its origins in aspects of life that provoke anxiety or insecurity, such as our ambivalence toward technology or our suspicion that beneath the veneer of normalcy lurk chaos and madness. Like the folk tale, its "orality" is short-lived, but the intriguing question arises as to whether the internet—often the favored means of transmission for urban legends—is itself part of the story, a kind of post-literate flux where the word is neither oral nor literate but shares qualities of both.

Today, the status and role of the storyteller are rather different; he or she is more often to be found in the rarefied atmosphere of library or classroom than in the lively informality of market-place or communal festivity. However, there is a difference between what we might term "formal" and "informal" entertainment. "Formal" entertainment is that which we consciously seek out for ourselves, generally at some expense, such as a visit to the cinema or theater. There is a clear and traditional separation between performer and audience, in which the latter plays a passive role as consumer, purchasing the professional services of the entertainer. The storyteller, by contrast, belongs to a more intimate environment than that of the auditorium. If we look at "informal" entertainment, however, we find ourselves in surroundings much more congenial to storytelling, because the grouping (as opposed to audience) is likely to be spontaneous and transitory, such as at a cafeteria table or a party. This is not to suggest that there will be an exchange of folk tales, but there may well be some storytelling, albeit of a very local and personal nature. Nevertheless, the point can be made that that's probably the way in which many tales originated; the great majority died as quickly as they were born, a few managed a brief existence, and a tiny number contained that mysterious seed of delight, universality, or wisdom that allowed them to beat the odds and survive.

What is emerging, then, is the fact that the fairy tale must be seen as a continuum. At one extreme we find the oral folk tale, which by its very nature cannot be represented in this book. As we have already observed, the oral tale's transformation into literary form requires careful analysis not only of the tale itself, but also of the motives and values of those responsible for its metamorphosis. At the other extreme there is the literary tale, written by a specific person at a specific time, which allows us readily to place the tale in its original context, as we might do in examining any other literary work. In between these two poles, however, we have an almost unlimited number of variations, as tradition blends with invention in the writer's mind. Given this wide range of possibilities, the more general term "fairy tale" is useful in its comprehensiveness.

The first two literary collections of fairy tales in the Western tradition are by

Italians whose names are relatively unknown outside scholarly circles: Giovanni Francesco Straparola (c. 1480-c. 1557), who published *The Facetious Nights* (1550), and Giambattista Basile (1575- 1632), the collector/writer of *The Pentamerone* (1634). Unfamiliar though these collections may be, they contain early versions of many tales that would later be made famous by Charles Perrault and the Grimm brothers. Both these men clearly recognized the vitality and appeal of folk tales and brought them to the attention of a literate *adult* audience, adapting and embellishing them as contemporary literary style and social taste demanded. Another similarity shared by these fairy-tale collections is that they are both built around a frame story—a third and celebrated example of which would arrive in the shape of Antoine Galland's translation into French of the *Arabian Nights* (1704).

Even before Perrault published his now-famous collection, the popularity of the fairy tale was growing among the French upper classes, who often gathered in fashionable "salons" to discuss matters of cultural and artistic interest. One outcome of these discussions was an enthusiasm—especially among aristocratic women such as Madame la Comtesse D'Aulnoy and Madame la Comtesse de Murat—for writing highly stylized literary tales based upon folk-tale models. Like Perrault, these aristocratic ladies saw the folk tale as in need of "improvement," and consequently their tales tell us a good deal about eighteenth-century aristocratic manners as well as present a "feminist" perspective that gives the tales a distinctly contemporary edge.

However, the most famous name among the French writer/collectors of fairy tales at the beginning of the eighteenth century was Charles Perrault (1628-1703). An influential government bureaucrat in Louis XIV's France, he was involved in a vigorous literary debate of the time known as the Quarrel of the Ancients and the Moderns, in which the "Ancients" were those who asserted the superiority of Classical literature and art, while the "Moderns" were of the view that contemporary works were pre-eminent, since they could draw on all the achievements of cultural and social progress. In publishing his collection of fairy tales, *Stories or Tales from Past Times, with Morals* (1697), Perrault made his Modernist credentials clear, since the tales were both French and very unclassical! Yet while this debate is now of interest only to literary historians, his introduction of these tales of the peasants into courtly society showed a little touch of genius. As the Opies observe, "The literary skill employed in the telling of the tales is universally acknowledged; yet it also appears that the tales were set down very largely as the writer heard them told."[1] At the same time, we should also assume that Perrault was familiar with the versions of these folk tales written by his predecessors Straparola and Basile—so that Perrault's particular achievement is one of synthesizing literary sophistication with oral simplicity. The

---

1   Iona and Peter Opie, *The Classic Fairy Tales* (London; Oxford UP, 1974) 21

daily lives of rural peasant and urban bourgeois (not to mention aristocrat) were literally worlds apart—and Perrault responded to that fact.

One hundred years later, the joint stimuli of nationalism and Romanticism were the driving forces behind the Grimm brothers' fascination with folk tales. At a time of great political and social upheaval, caused first by French occupation and then by the process of unification as the modern Germany was being forged out of a patchwork of tiny states and principalities, there was a growing need to answer a new question: what does it mean to be German? At the same time, they were responding to the contemporary Romantic creed that the true spirit of a people was to be found not in the palaces or even the cities, but in the countryside, far away from urban sophistication. Jacob and Wilhelm Grimm (1785-1863; 1786-1859) might be described as archaeologists of a sort—although contrary to what was once believed, they were rarely if ever involved with any "digs" that first discovered these tales among the unlettered country folk. Such is the preeminence of the Grimms' collection *Tales for Young and Old* (first published 1812-15) that we tend to regard it as being almost as organic and timeless a phenomenon as the tales themselves. It is nevertheless a fact that in more recent times, controversy has swirled around the Grimms' methodology and motivation in assembling their collection. The image of the brothers roaming the German countryside, gathering the tales in remote villages and hamlets, is attractive but false; generally, they were contributed by literate, middle-class friends and relatives, who thus represent yet another intermediary stage between the genuine folk tale, on the one hand, and the literary tale on the other. Indeed, the claim made by the Grimms in the Preface to the Second Edition of their tales (1819)—"... we have not embellished any detail or feature of the story told itself, but rather rendered its content just as we received it."[1]—appears confusing, given ample evidence to the contrary. We should not forget, however, that the scholarly brothers were pioneers in revising these tales for an audience radically different from the illiterate country folk amongst whom they originated. Ralph Manheim, the translator of the Grimm tales in this anthology, asserts that the brothers' genius was in "mak[ing] us hear the voices of the individual storytellers ... In the German text the human voice takes on a wide variety of tones ... But everywhere—or almost—it is a natural human voice, speaking as someone might speak ..."[2] And once their popularity among children became apparent, Wilhelm in particular assumed the responsibility of ensuring that the tales were made suitable for the eyes of the child, according to contemporary notions about children's reading.

---

1 Joyce Crick, *Jacob and Wilhelm Grimm Selected Tales* (Oxford UP, 2005) 8. See also Zohar Shavit, *Poetics of Children's Literature* (Athens, GA and London: U of Georgia P, 1986) 20-27.

2 Ralph Manheim, *Grimms' Tales for Young and Old* (New York, 1977), Translator's Preface, 1.

Even when we come to the tales of Hans Christian Andersen (1805-75), the link with folk tale remains strong. We perceive Andersen as a writer of original fairy tales rather than as a collector, and we assume, therefore, that his tales were exclusively of his own invention. What we need to consider is that Andersen came from a poor, working-class background in which the oral folk tale was common currency; consequently, his imagination was well primed before ever the world of literacy opened up new vistas of fancy to him. So it is hardly surprising to discover that several of Andersen's better-known tales (such as "The Tinderbox" and "The Princess and the Pea") either allude to, or are retellings of, traditional stories—some that he heard, and some that he later read. We should bear in mind that Andersen was barely a generation younger than the Grimm brothers and was well-acquainted with them; ironically, it appears that on at least one occasion, the folk tale owed a debt to Andersen: the Opies remind us that in 1843 the Grimms published a tale that closely resembled "The Princess and the Pea." However, Andersen's literary contribution to the fairy tale differs from that of the Grimms in the sense that while the latter were primarily concerned with presenting their tales in the most acceptable form to the German people, Andersen had a much more personal involvement with his tales. In his hands, a tale, whatever its source, became yet another opportunity for self-revelation. (It is no coincidence that he entitled one of his autobiographies *The Fairytale of My Life*.) As we have already seen, a knowledge of the historical context of the tales adds an extra dimension to our appreciation of them; in the case of Andersen and the other fairy-tale writers, that aspect becomes more specific, in the sense that we can now place the tales in a personal context as well as a social one.

The fact is that some rather unlikely minds have been drawn to express themselves through fairy tale, suggesting that the form retains a freedom and an energy that has survived the transformation of audience from rural simplicity to urban sophistication. What attraction could the fairy tale possibly have had for such an apparently worldly individual as Oscar Wilde (1854-1900), for instance? Yet his tales (*The Happy Prince* and *The Selfish Giant* are the best-known examples) show a great deal of craft and attention to detail, which suggests that they meant more to him than mere occasional pieces. Wilde, like other well-known nineteenth-century writers such as George MacDonald, John Ruskin, and even Charles Dickens, regarded the fairy tale as one of many literary forms to choose from, with its own particular advantages and limitations.

There is no question, however, that these writers (with the possible exception of Wilde) saw their primary audience as children—in several cases, their tales were composed with specific children in mind. Even Charles Perrault, at the end of the seventeenth century, had some awareness of the appeal of fairy tales for children, as is indicated by the frontispiece of the 1697 edition of his tales, with its inscription

"Contes de ma Mère L'Oye" ("Tales of Mother Goose") and its depiction of an old woman spinning while she spins her yarn (!) to a group of children. The assumption is extended by his addition of explicit morals to the tales, thus making them overtly cautionary in nature. It is the narrator's ironic tone and occasional comment that betray his interest in appealing to an older, more sophisticated audience.

In England, the presence of the fairy tale in children's literature of the eighteenth century likewise depended on its ability to provide moral instruction. With its fantastic and sometimes violent and amoral content, the fairy tale was disapproved of by both the upholders of Puritan attitudes and the growing advocates of a more rational outlook, exemplified in the philosophy and influential educational theories of John Locke. In their efforts to provide children with stories of virtue and piety, both the Rational Moralists and Sunday School Moralists of the late eighteenth and nineteenth centuries also looked upon this popular literature with a consternation verging on horror. In the periodical *The Guardian of Education*, its editor, the influential Sarah Trimmer, warned parents and governesses of the dangers of fairy tales: "A moment's consideration will surely be sufficient to convince people of the least reflection, of the danger, as well as the impropriety, of putting such books as these into the hands of little children, whose minds are susceptible to every impression; and who from the liveliness of their imaginations are apt to convert into realities whatever forcibly strikes their fancy."[1]

Despite this persistent disapproval, however, the tales were made available to eighteenth-century children through a somewhat less "respectable" source of reading material—chapbooks. The purveyors of this popular literature would not have had the scruples of the more reputable publishers, such as John Newbery, who sought to uphold the current educational theories of Locke. Chapbook publishers recognized the attraction of tales of fantasy and imagination and sought to provide them cheaply—generally by means of traveling peddlers—to the folk, child and adult alike. Thus the folk tale had, in a sense, come full circle. In being written down, it had been taken from the illiterate folk; now, as literacy was spreading slowly through the population, the tale could be returned—at a price—from whence it came.

During the early years of the nineteenth century, the Romantics would counter the prevailing criticism of fairy tales and denounce the moralizing and utilitarian books that were being produced for children. In his affirmation of the value of fantasy in his early reading, the poet Samuel Taylor Coleridge reacted against the common disapproval of such literature:

---

1 Sarah Trimmer, "Nursery Tales," in *The Guardian of Education* 4 (1805) 74-75, as quoted in *Children and Literature: Views and Reviews*, ed. Virginia Haviland (Glenview, IL: Scott and Foresman, 1973) 7.

"Should children be permitted to read Romances, and Relations of Giants and Magicians and Genii?—I know all that has been said against it; but I have formed my faith in the affirmative—I know no other way of giving the mind a love of 'the great' and 'the Whole.'"[1]

Although resistance to the fairy tale continued throughout the nineteenth century, when Grimms' fairy tales appeared in England in 1823, they were immediately popular. In the preface to his translation of the tales, Edgar Taylor criticized, in Romantic fashion, the prevailing educational goals and defended the value of fairy stories: "philosophy is made the companion of the nursery; we have lisping chemists and leading-string mathematicians ... Our imagination is surely as susceptible of improvement by exercise as our judgement and our memory."[2] His one stricture on imaginative stories was that they not interfere with moral education. Despite the acceptance of the Grimm brothers' work, it would be another twenty years before the fairy tale was fully accepted as literature for children. During the 1840s, the translation into English of Andersen's literary tales gave rise to the publication of a number of fairy-tale collections which reached its apogee almost fifty years later in Andrew Lang's "color" series, beginning with the *Blue Fairy Book* (1889). After the success of the Grimms' tales, the arrival of Andersen's work represented an important next step in the restitution of the fairy-tale, although disapproving voices could still be heard. As Jack Zipes observes, "[Andersen's] unusual tales, which combined fantasy with a moral impulse in line with traditional Christian standards, guaranteed the legitimacy of the literary fairy tale for middle-class audiences."[3] Thus, after centuries of criticism and banishment to the trade of the chapman, fairy tales and fantasy finally achieved the status which they have never since lost—that of "approved" literature for children.

The second half of the nineteenth century witnessed the period that is often referred to as the Golden Age of children's literature. It may also have been the time when the lines became blurred as to just what constituted a fairy tale, since many of the works published for children were fantasies, beginning with Lewis Carroll's *Alice's Adventures in Wonderland* (1865)—and as we have already noted, Carroll himself referred to its sequel *Through the Looking-Glass* (1871) as a fairy tale. Be that as it may, the fairy tale evolved in several ways: it grew longer (as in the work of writers such as George MacDonald and Andrew Lang), more didactic (Charles Kingsley's *The Water Babies* (1863) and the stories of Mary Louisa Molesworth are examples),

1 Earl Leslie Griggs, ed., *Collected Letters of Samuel Taylor Coleridge, 1785-1800* (Oxford: Clarendon P, 1956) 1:354.
2 Edgar Taylor, ed., *German Popular Stories* (London: John Camden Hotten, 1869) 90.
3 Jack Zipes, *Victorian Fairy Tales* (New York, 1987), Introduction, xviii.

and more focussed upon social issues. Indeed, this last point raises an interesting paradox in the literary tale's evolution from the folk tale. Despite the *collective* nature of the folk tale's composition, its concerns are generally those of the individual, such as growing up, establishing a relationship, and so on. When we turn to the literary tale, it is attributable to a *single* writer but now tends to deal with social (i.e., collective) subjects.

However, in the process of becoming so closely associated with children, fairy tales have all too often been dismissed as literature not worthy of serious attention on the part of adult readers. In his pioneering essay "On Fairy Stories," J.R.R. Tolkien, author of the fantasy works *The Hobbit* and *Lord of the Rings*, was among the first to point out that this association of fairy stories with children is a historical accident and that children "neither like fairy stories more, nor understand them better than adults do; and no more than they like other things."[1] Tolkien saw fairy stories as a natural branch of literature, sharing the same qualities as may be found in many other genres.

It certainly can be argued that the fairy tale has regained an adult audience in recent times. The surprise is in the fact that these tales have been out of favor for so long among older readers, since fairy tales present us with both adult and child triumphing over their (and our) deepest fears and desires. Perhaps we have been the victims of our own rationalistic preconceptions of what a fairy tale actually is and what it has to say to us. The child psychologist Bruno Bettelheim's observation that at each stage of our lives, fairy tales take on new significance and speak "simultaneously to all levels of the human personality, communicating in a manner which reaches the uneducated mind of the child as well as that of the sophisticated adult"[2] was hardly a revelation in itself, but the impact that his book *The Uses of Enchantment: The Meaning and Importance of Fairy Tales* made when it was published in 1976 suggested that the time was ripe for a reappraisal—a project that has produced a substantial body of scholarship.

This recognition of the ability of the fairy tale to appeal to both child and adult has resulted in a recent resurgence of publications that address both audiences. A quick survey of any bookstore will reveal a number of shelves in the children's section devoted to fairy tales. They will doubtless include classic tales by Perrault, the Grimms, and Andersen, most likely in the form of lavishly illustrated individual works. Also available will be versions that reflect a particular motivation in their tellers—feminist, psychological, or environmental, for instance—whose approach ranges from parody to realism. Nearby the browser will come across shelves devoted

---

1   J.R.R. Tolkien, "On Fairy Stories," in *Tree and Leaf* (London: George Allen and Unwin, 1977) 38.
2   Bruno Bettelheim, *The Uses of Enchantment: The Meaning and Importance of Fairy Tales* (New York: Alfred Knopf, 1976) 5-6.

to novel-length retellings intended for the young-adult reader (female in particular) by authors such as Jane Yolen, Robin McKinley, and Donna Jo Napoli, whose work—not surprisingly—tends to focus upon those tales that deal with the challenges of growing up. The fairy tale can also be found in a new and expanding section of the bookstore given over to the Graphic Novel. The publishing term may be new, the quality improved, and the cost higher, but the format is still that of the humble comic book. It should come as no surprise to find the classic tales represented here, as their brevity, simplicity, and concreteness are qualities ideally suited to the graphic novel. Inroads have also been made into adult fiction; several well-known novelists (Margaret Atwood, A.S. Byatt, and Gregory Maguire among them) have acknowledged the deep and abiding influence that fairy tales have had on their own writing. And for those who remain unconvinced about how deeply embedded the fairy tale is in our collective unconscious, we note that on more specialized shelves in our hypothetical bookstore may be found such titles as *From Cinderella to CEO: How to Master the 10 Lessons of Fairy Tales to Transform Your Work Life* (2005), *Teaching Thinking Skills with Fairy Tales and Fantasy* (2005)—or even *Erotic Fairy Tales: A Romp Through the Classics* (2001). What emerges is that the fairy tale remains as relevant, democratic, and adaptable as it has ever been in its long history.

Without a doubt, however, the most significant development for the fairy tale (and for culture in general) in the twentieth century has come from the film medium. The screening of *Snow White and the Seven Dwarves* in 1937 initiated the phenomenal influence that the Walt Disney studios have exerted upon our experience of the fairy tale. Seventy years and numerous films later, the animated Disney fairy tale is the first, and often only, version with which North Americans are familiar. For better or for worse—like all storytellers, collectors, and re-writers—Walt Disney has put his own imprint upon the tales. However, unlike his predecessors, he chose to combine the power of the film medium with the Disney entertainment empire (Disney World and Disneyland and Euro-Disney, where we can meet and dine with Cinderella and Sleeping Beauty), to both disseminate and consolidate his vision to an unprecedented degree. Although Disney's influence has provoked fierce criticism (see Betsy Hearne's article), it is only recently, (through the medium of film, of course), that Disney's twentieth-century hegemony over the fairy tale has been challenged. Replacing Disney's royal romances are the sophisticated fractured fairy tales such as the *Shrek* series (2001, 2004, 2007, 2010) and *Hoodwinked* (2005) (see James Poniewozik's article). Disney's apparently unassailable pairing of fairy tale and animation has now been broadened to include "realistic" fairy-tale films such as *Ever After* (1998) or *Pan's Labyrinth* (2006) and fantasy television shows such as *The Tenth Kingdom* (2000). Not surprisingly, the wide range of approaches to be found in contemporary books is paralleled in the medium of film. Yet as the example of

Disney's influence so clearly demonstrates, film and television have emerged as the current media of popular culture. In so doing (criticism of Disney notwithstanding), they have made the fairy tale very much a part of mass culture just as it once was a part of folk culture; in this respect, the folk tale has come full circle.

One essential feature that has hopefully been established in this introduction, and that will be confirmed in the sections that follow, is that fairy tales can come in a bewildering number of versions. It begins with the infinite variability of the oral folk tale, continues with the differing assumptions or agendas of collectors, translators, and editors as the tale takes on literary form, and then undergoes constant transformation as generations of writers and illustrators are drawn to this mother-lode of story. Exploring the world of fairy tale, therefore, becomes rather a different kind of challenge than reading a nineteenth-century novel, for instance. While we may choose to read other works by the same author or historical texts to understand the context of the novel, the fact remains that we are dealing with just one novel. That is rarely the case with the fairy tale—and so to base a theory on the evidence of one version alone may well be to build a house of cards, for who is to say that this version is more authentic than any other? In some cases it may be possible to demonstrate that a particular version is the oldest of known variants—but is age the only criterion? Is it even possible to think of one specific version of a folk tale as definitive? Thus, any theory that we may devise applies in the first instance only to one version of a particular tale; the challenge then is to see if it retains its validity on being applied to other versions and even other tales.[1]

---

1   See Alan Dundes's fuller discussion of this issue in his article "Fairy Tales from a Folkloristic Perspective," in Ruth Bottigheimer, ed., *Fairy Tales and Society: Illusion, Allusion and Paradigm* (Philadelphia: U of Pennsylvania P, 1986).

LITTLE RED RIDING HOOD

FOR WHAT IS UNQUESTIONABLY ONE of the classic fairy tales, "Little Red Riding Hood" is more surprising for what it lacks than for what it contains. There is no royalty, no enchantment, no romance—just a talking wolf with a big appetite. How then has the heroine of this tale become as famous a figure as her more glamorous cousins, Sleeping Beauty, Cinderella, and Snow White? What is so remarkable about this stark little tale that describes the dramatic confrontation between an innocent little girl and a wicked wolf? How has it come about that the line "Grandmother, what big teeth you have!" is one of the most anticipated and familiar moments in all of Western literature, let alone fairy tale?

First of all, this is not a real wolf—and arguably neither child nor adult reader ever takes him as such. The first story in this section actually identifies him as a "bzou" or werewolf ("wer" is Old English for "man"), and, as Jack Zipes points out in his discussion of this version in *The Trials and Tribulations of Little Red Riding Hood*,

> The direct forebears of Perrault's literary tale were not influenced by sun worship or Christian theology, but by the very material conditions of their existence and traditional pagan superstition. Little children were attacked and killed by animals and grownups in the woods and fields. Hunger often drove people to commit atrocious acts. In the 15th and 16th centuries, violence was difficult to explain on rational grounds. There was a strong superstitious belief in werewolves and witches, uncontrollable magical forces of nature, which threatened the lives of the peasant population.... Consequently, the warning tale became part of a stock oral repertoire of storytellers.[1]

---

1 Jack D. Zipes, ed., *The Trials and Tribulations of Little Red Riding Hood*, 2nd ed. (New York: Routledge, 1993) 18-20.

Although it was only recorded in 1885, scholars are in general agreement that "The Story of Grandmother" is likely very similar to the version that Perrault heard two hundred years earlier. There are several intriguing aspects to this early version of the tale. The representation of the two paths through the forest as being of needles and pins is no doubt a play on the pine needles that carpet the forest floor; it may also be a sly reference to one of the domestic tasks that awaits feminine maturity. This tale also has a crudeness that underlines its folk origins—a conclusion borne out by the fact that variants from other parts of the world contain similar scatological episodes. Paul Delarue, the editor of the collection from which this tale was taken, observes in his notes that "... the common elements that are lacking in [Perrault's] story are precisely those which would have shocked the society of his period by their cruelness [sic] ... and their impropriety."[1]

Thus, what we see in Perrault's version is the adaptation of a gross folk tale to the more sophisticated tastes of high society. He removes all overt human aspects of his antagonist, relying simply on the powerful archetypal image of the wolf as predator and interloper. By way of compensation for his excision of the tale's vulgarities, Perrault appears to be responsible for the artistic touch of the red riding hood; he would doubtless be both shocked and amused to learn how controversial an addition that turned out to be! He tells us that it's a "hood like the ones that fine ladies wear when they go riding," which suggests that he's again trying to link the tale with the world of his audience—but why is it *red*? We are confronted with a color symbolic of sexuality that provides a further hint about Perrault's own assumptions regarding this tale.

The ending of "The Story of Grandmother" catches our eye because its happy outcome is attributable to the girl's practical quick-wittedness—a quality that Perrault denies his heroine, in keeping with his bourgeois assumptions about female naïvety and vulnerability, which makes Little Red Riding Hood into the wolf's unwitting accomplice. Perrault's tragic and presumably truncated ending, which catches the modern reader so much by surprise, goes against folk-tale custom, but it is clear that such an ending suited Perrault's purposes admirably, given the Moral that he appended to the tale: "Children, especially pretty, nicely brought-up young ladies, ought never to talk to strangers ..." Just what induced Perrault to add his Morals to the tales is unclear, but it was surely a critical moment in the evolution of the fairy tale as children's literature; to this day, the belief has persisted that the purpose of a tale is to inculcate morals into young minds. We must remember that Perrault was a pioneer in recognizing the potential appeal of these tales and transforming them from an oral into a literary form. As Jack Zipes points out,

---

1   Paul Delarue, comp., *Borzoi Book of French Folk Tales*, trans. Austin E. Fife (New York: Knopf, 1956).

Perrault's tale of "Little Red Riding Hood" had an unusually successful reception in the 18th century. In fact, it was one of the few literary tales in history which, due to its universality, ambivalence, and clever sexual innuendos, was reabsorbed by the oral folk tradition. That is, as a result of its massive circulation in print in the 18th and 19th centuries and of the corroboration of peasant experience, it took root in oral folklore and eventually led to the creation of the even more popular Grimms' tale, which had the same effect.[1]

When we turn to the Grimms' version, published over a hundred years later, we find a synthesis of the other two, with some intriguing additions. (Despite the Grimms' insistence that they were capturing the essence of the German spirit in their tales, it is surely not coincidental that the family that contributed this tale was of French extraction.) The red garment remains, as does the wolf; like Perrault, the Grimms choose to gloss over the cannibalistic snack that the girl unwittingly makes of her grandmother, and the "happy" ending has been restored—but only through the intervention of the paternalistic hunter, in a scene derived, according to Paul Delarue, from another French tale, "The Goat and Her Kids."

Nevertheless, it can be argued that the Grimm version is the most balanced, at least to the contemporary reader. The hunter presents an image of male goodness that counters the male wickedness of the wolf; the mother appears concerned about her daughter's correct behavior, if not her welfare—and the less familiar appended story, describing the defeat of a second wolf through the strategy of a wiser girl and grandmother, sends a very different message from Perrault's harsh ending, reminding us that, having realized the popularity of their tales among children, the Grimms endeavored to select and edit them with desirable educational principles in mind.

The story of Little Red Riding Hood has for so long been an inescapable part of growing up in the English language that it is hard enough to contemplate its greater authenticity in French or German. It comes as an even greater shock, therefore, to realize how old and widespread the tale is in Asia; Delarue points out that versions of the tale are widely distributed in China, Japan, and Korea.[2]

"The Chinese Red Riding Hoods" also reveals significant structural differences, but, on closer examination, we may be surprised to discover just how many of the elements from the previous versions are to be found here: as in "The Story of Grandmother," the children escape from the wolf's clutches by means of a clever ruse, and his final demise is brought about by much the same strategy as in the conclusion to

---

1   Zipes, *The Trials and Tribulations* 31.
2   In Alan Dundes, ed., *Little Red Riding Hood: A Casebook* (Madison, WI: U of Wisconsin P, 1989) 13.

"Little Red Cap"—that is, by exploiting the greed and self-indulgence that are central to the fairy-tale wolf's character.

In some respects, this Chinese version has a distinctly contemporary feel. The mother is described as a young widow who teaches her children carefully about the nature of the world; yet the time must come when her children will have to fend for themselves—and at that moment of crisis, the girls prove susceptible to the wolf's trickery. Despite their mistake, however, the sisters (led by the formidable Felice) are able to keep their wits about them and finally outsmart the deceitful wolf. The experience may have deprived them of at least some of their trust in those around them; by the same token, they will be less likely to be fooled a second time.

What is intriguing about "Flossie and the Fox," by Patricia McKissack, is that it presents us with yet another central character who, like her Chinese counterparts, follows in the female trickster tradition that emerged in "The Story of Grandmother." Not surprisingly, this tale too is close to the oral tradition, as McKissack explains in her Author's Note. Indeed, the setting of the rural American South may remind us of a considerably more notorious mischief-maker in the shape of Brer Rabbit—not least because Flossie's would-be antagonist is a rather supercilious fox instead of a wolf. The fact that Flossie has the situation fully under control signifies a complete reversal of the message of female helplessness that infuses Perrault's tale.

The concern with the suitability of the fairy tale for a younger audience, which began with Perrault and became increasingly a concern for the Grimms with each subsequent edition of their tales, is even more apparent in contemporary re-workings. A good example is to be found in the popular work of American writer-illustrator David McPhail. His adherence to the traditional non-specific setting ensures that his version (1995) is easily accessible, Little Red Riding Hood is clever and resourceful, the Wolf is outsmarted in comic fashion with no one getting hurt, and the moral messages are communicated without a hint of the violence and underlying sexuality that are so much a part of earlier versions of the tale. The goal, as the book jacket claims, is to provide "tales that are perfect for today's very young child."

To this point, all the versions of Little Red Riding Hood have been set in rural surroundings, as befits their origins. The modern world, however, is essentially an urban one, and that fact is reflected in Francesca Lia Block's "Wolf" (2000), which takes place, at least in part, in the concrete jungle of Los Angeles. (Sarah Moon uses the medium of photography in much the same context, see p. 140). For the first time, the story is told from the girl's point of view (although Block has chosen to add some years to her central character whose age, the "Little" in her name notwithstanding, has been ambiguous from the beginning). With this story of abuse, loneliness, and misery, we have come a long way from the fairy-tale world of Little Red Riding Hood, and yet the dark shadows are visible from the beginning; the fact that writers have chosen to peer more and more closely into that darkness says something both about us and about the remarkable potency of this encounter between a girl and a wolf.

THE STORY OF GRANDMOTHER[1]

Paul Delarue

THERE WAS ONCE A WOMAN who had some bread, and she said to her daughter: "You are going to carry a hot loaf and a bottle of milk to your grandmother."

The little girl departed. At the crossroads she met the *bzou*, who said to her: "Where are you going?"

"I'm taking a hot loaf and a bottle of milk to my grandmother."

"What road are you taking," said the *bzou*, "the Needles Road or the Pins Road?" "The Needles Road," said the little girl.

"Well, I shall take the Pins Road."

The little girl enjoyed herself picking up needles. Meanwhile the *bzou* arrived at her grandmother's, killed her, put some of her flesh in the pantry and a bottle of her blood on the shelf. The little girl arrived and knocked at the door.

"Push the door," said the *bzou*, "it's closed with a wet straw."

"Hello, Grandmother; I'm bringing you a hot loaf and a bottle of milk."

"Put them in the pantry. You eat the meat that's in it and drink a bottle of wine that is on the shelf."

As she ate there was a little cat that said: "A slut is she who eats the flesh and drinks the blood of her grandmother!"

"Undress, my child," said the *bzou*, "and come and sleep beside me."

"Where should I put my apron?"

"Throw it in the fire, my child; you don't need it any more."

"Where should I put my bodice?"

"Throw it in the fire, my child; you don't need it any more."

"Where should I put my dress?"

"Throw it in the fire, my child; you don't need it any more."

"Where should I put my skirt?"

"Throw it in the fire, my child; you don't need it any more."

---

[1] First collected in 1885; this text from Delarue, *The Borzoi Book of French Folktales*, trans. Austin E. Fife (New York: Knopf, 1956).

"Where should I put my hose?"

"Throw it in the fire, my child; you don't need it any more."

"Oh, Grandmother, how hairy you are!"

"It's to keep me warmer, my child."

"Oh, Grandmother, those long nails you have!"

"It's to scratch me better, my child!"

"Oh, Grandmother, those big shoulders that you have!"

"All the better to carry kindling from the woods, my child."

"Oh, Grandmother, those big ears that you have!"

"All the better to hear with, my child."

"Oh, Grandmother, that big mouth you have!"

"All the better to eat you with, my child!"

"Oh, Grandmother, I need to go outside to relieve myself."

"Do it in the bed, my child."

"Oh, Grandmother, I want to go outside."

"All right, but don't stay long."

The *bzou* tied a woolen thread to her foot and let her go out, and when the little girl was outside she tied the end of the string to a big plum tree in the yard. The *bzou* got impatient and said:

"Are you making cables?"

When he became aware that no one answered him, he jumped out of bed and saw that the little girl had escaped. He followed her, but he arrived at her house just at the moment she was safely inside.

LITTLE RED RIDING HOOD[1]

Charles Perrault

O NCE UPON A TIME, DEEP in the heart of the country, there lived a pretty little girl whose mother adored her, and her grandmother adored her even more. This good woman made her a red hood like the ones that fine ladies wear when they go riding. The hood suited the child so much that soon everybody was calling her Little Red Riding Hood.

---

1   First published in 1697. This text from *Sleeping Beauty and Other Favourite Fairy Tales,* trans. Angela Carter (London: Gollancz, 1982).

One day, her mother baked some cakes on the griddle and said to Little Red Riding Hood:

"Your granny is sick; you must go and visit her. Take her one of these cakes and a little pot of butter."

Little Red Riding Hood went off to the next village to visit her grandmother. As she walked through the wood, she met a wolf, who wanted to eat her but did not dare to because there were woodcutters working nearby. He asked her where she was going. The poor child did not know how dangerous it is to chatter away to wolves and replied innocently:

"I'm going to visit my grandmother to take her this cake and this little pot of butter from my mother."

"Does your grandmother live far away?" asked the wolf.

"Oh yes," said Little Red Riding Hood. "She lives beyond the mill you can see over there, in the first house you come to in the village."

"Well, I shall go and visit her, too," said the wolf. "I will take *this* road and you shall take *that* road and let's see who can get there first."

The wolf ran off by the shortest path and Red Riding Hood went off the longest way and she made it still longer because she dawdled along, gathering nuts and chasing butterflies and picking bunches of wayside flowers.

The wolf soon arrived at Grandmother's house. He knocked on the door, rat tat tat.

"Who's there?"

"Your granddaughter, Little Red Riding Hood," said the wolf, disguising his voice. "I've brought you a cake baked on the griddle and a little pot of butter from my mother."

Grandmother was lying in bed because she was poorly. She called out: "Lift up the latch and walk in!"

The wolf lifted the latch and opened the door. He had not eaten for three days. He threw himself on the good woman and gobbled her up. Then he closed the door behind him and lay down in Grandmother's bed to wait for Little Red Riding Hood. At last she came knocking on the door, rat tat tat.

"Who's there?"

Little Red Riding Hood heard the hoarse voice of the wolf and thought that her grandmother must have caught a cold. She answered:

"It's your granddaughter, Little Red Riding Hood. I've brought you a cake baked on the griddle and a little pot of butter from my mother."

The wolf disguised his voice and said:

"Lift up the latch and walk in."

Little Red Riding Hood lifted the latch and opened the door.

When the wolf saw her come in, he hid himself under the bedclothes and said to her:

"Put the cake and the butter down on the bread-bin and come and lie down with me."

Little Red Riding Hood took off her clothes and went to lie down in the bed. She was surprised to see how odd her grandmother looked. She said to her:

"Grandmother, what big arms you have!"

"All the better to hold you with, my dear."

"Grandmother, what big legs you have!"

"All the better to run with, my dear."

"Grandmother, what big ears you have!"

"All the better to hear with, my dear."

"Grandmother, what big eyes you have!"

"All the better to see with, my dear!"

"Grandmother, what big teeth you have!"

"All the better to eat you up!"

At that, the wicked wolf threw himself upon Little Red Riding Hood and gobbled her up, too.

Moral

Children, especially pretty, nicely brought-up young ladies, ought never to talk to strangers; if they are foolish enough to do so, they should not be surprised if some greedy wolf consumes them, elegant red riding hoods and all.

Now, there are real wolves, with hairy pelts and enormous teeth; but also wolves who seem perfectly charming, sweet-natured and obliging, who pursue young girls in the street and pay them the most flattering attentions.

Unfortunately, these smooth-tongued, smooth-pelted wolves are the most dangerous beasts of all.

LITTLE RED CAP[1]

Jacob and Wilhelm Grimm

ONCE THERE WAS A DEAR little girl whom everyone loved. Her grandmother loved her most of all and didn't know what to give the child next. Once she gave her a little red velvet cap, which was so becoming to her that she never wanted to wear anything else, and that was why everyone called her Little Red Cap. One day her mother said: "Look, Little Red Cap, here's a piece of cake and a bottle of wine. Take them to grandmother. She is sick and weak, and they will make her feel better. You'd better start now before it gets too hot; walk properly like a good little girl, and don't leave the path or you'll fall down and break the bottle and there won't be anything for grandmother. And when you get to her house, don't forget to say good morning, and don't go looking in all the corners."

"I'll do everything right," Little Red Cap promised her mother. Her grandmother lived in the wood, half an hour's walk from the village. No sooner had Little Red Cap set foot in the wood than she met the wolf. But Little Red Cap didn't know what a wicked beast he was, so she wasn't afraid of him. "Good morning, Little Red Cap," he said. "Thank you kindly, wolf." "Where are you going so early, Little Red Cap?" "To my grandmother's." "And what's that you've got under your apron?" "Cake and wine. We baked yesterday, and we want my grandmother, who's sick and weak, to have something nice that will make her feel better." "Where does your grandmother live, Little Red Cap?" "In the wood, fifteen or twenty minutes' walk from here, under the three big oak trees. That's where the house is. It has hazel hedges around it. You must know the place." "How young and tender she is!" thought the wolf. "Why, she'll be even tastier than the old woman. Maybe if I'm crafty enough I can get them both." So, after walking along for a short while beside Little Red Cap, he said: "Little Red Cap, open your eyes. What lovely flowers! Why don't you look around you? I don't believe you even hear how sweetly the birds are singing. It's so gay out here in the wood, yet you trudge along as solemnly as if you were going to school."

Little Red Cap looked up, and when she saw the sunbeams dancing this way and that between the trees and the beautiful flowers all around her, she thought: "Grandmother will be pleased if I bring her a bunch of nice fresh flowers. It's so early now that I'm sure to be there in plenty of time." So she left the path and went into the wood to pick flowers. And when she had picked one, she thought there must be a

---

1   First published in 1812/15, in the first edition of *Kinder- und Hausmärchen*. This text from the second edition (1819), from *Grimms' Tales for Young and Old*, trans. Ralph Manheim (Garden City, NY: Anchor P, 1977).

more beautiful one farther on, so she went deeper and deeper into the wood. As for the wolf, he went straight to the grandmother's house and knocked at the door. "Who's there?" "Little Red Cap, bringing cake and wine. Open the door." "Just raise the latch," cried the grandmother, "I'm too weak to get out of bed." The wolf raised the latch and the door swung open. Without saying a single word he went straight to the grandmother's bed and gobbled her up. Then he put on her clothes and her nightcap, lay down in the bed, and drew the curtains.

Meanwhile Little Red Cap had been running about picking flowers, and when she had as many as she could carry she remembered her grandmother and started off again. She was surprised to find the door open, and when she stepped into the house she had such a strange feeling that she said to herself: "My goodness, I'm usually so glad to see grandmother. Why am I frightened today?" "Good morning," she cried out, but there was no answer. Then she went to the bed and opened the curtains. The grandmother had her cap pulled way down over her face, and looked very strange.

"Oh, grandmother, what big ears you have!"

"The better to hear you with."

"Oh, grandmother, what big eyes you have!"

"The better to see you with."

"Oh, grandmother, what big hands you have!"

"The better to grab you with."

"But, grandmother, what a dreadful big mouth you have!"

"The better to eat you with."

And no sooner had the wolf spoken than he bounded out of bed and gobbled up poor Little Red Cap.

When the wolf had stilled his hunger, he got back into bed, fell asleep, and began to snore very very loud. A hunter was just passing, and he thought: "How the old woman is snoring! I'd better go and see what's wrong." So he stepped into the house and went over to the bed and saw the wolf was in it. "You old sinner!" he said, "I've found you at last. It's been a long time." He levelled his musket and was just about to fire when it occurred to him that the wolf might have swallowed the grandmother and that there might still be a chance of saving her. So instead of firing, he took a pair of scissors and started cutting the sleeping wolf's belly open. After two snips, he saw the little red cap, and after another few snips the little girl jumped out, crying: "Oh, I've been so afraid! It was so dark inside the wolf!" And then the old grandmother came out, and she too was still alive, though she could hardly breathe. Little Red Cap ran outside and brought big stones, and they filled the wolf's belly with them. When he woke up, he wanted to run away, but the stones were so heavy that his legs wouldn't carry him and he fell dead.

All three were happy; the hunter skinned the wolf and went home with the skin; the grandmother ate the cake and drank the wine Little Red Cap had brought her and soon got well; and as for Little Red Cap, she said to herself: "Never again will I leave the path and run off into the wood when my mother tells me not to."

Another story they tell is that when Little Red Cap was taking another cake to her old grandmother another wolf spoke to her and tried to make her leave the path. But Little Red Cap was on her guard. She kept on going, and when she got to her grandmother's she told her how she had met a wolf who had bidden her good day but given her such a wicked look that "if it hadn't been on the open road he'd have gobbled me right up." "Well then," said the grandmother, "we'll just lock the door and he won't be able to get in." In a little while the wolf knocked and called out: "Open the door, grandmother, it's Little Red Cap. I've brought you some cake." But they didn't say a word and they didn't open the door. So Grayhead circled the house once or twice and finally jumped on the roof. His plan was to wait until evening when Little Red Cap would go home, and then he'd creep after her and gobble her up in the darkness. But the grandmother guessed what he had in mind. There was a big stone trough in front of the house, and she said to the child: "Here's a bucket, Little Red Cap. I cooked some sausages yesterday. Take the water I cooked them in and empty it into the trough." Little Red Cap carried water until the trough was full. The smell of the sausages rose up to the wolf's nostrils. He sniffed and looked down, and in the end he stuck his neck out so far that he couldn't keep his footing and began to slide. And he slid off the roof and slid straight into the big trough and was drowned. And Little Red Cap went happily home, and no one harmed her.

THE CHINESE RED RIDING HOODS[1]

Isabelle C. Chang

"Beware of the wolf in sheep's clothing."

MANY YEARS AGO IN CHINA there lived a young widow with her three children. On their grandmother's birthday, the mother went to visit her.

"Felice," she cautioned her oldest daughter before she left, "you must watch over your sisters Mayling and Jeanne while I am gone. Lock the door and don't let anyone inside. I shall be back tomorrow."

---

1   From *Chinese Fairy Tales* (Barre, MA: Barre Publishers, 1965).

A wolf who was hiding near the house at the edge of the woods overheard the news.

When it was dark he disguised himself as an elderly woman and knocked at the door of the three girls' house.

"Who is it?" called Felice.

"Felice, Mayling, and Jeanne, my treasures, it is your Grammie," answered the wolf as sweetly as possible.

"Grammie," said Felice through the door, "Mummy just went to see you!"

"It is too bad I missed her. We must have taken different roads," replied the crafty wolf.

"Grammie," asked Mayling, "why is your voice so different tonight?"

"Your old Grammie caught cold and is hoarse. Please let me in quickly, for it is drafty out here and the night air is very bad for me."

The tender-hearted girls could not bear to keep their grandmother out in the cold, so they unlatched the door and shouted, "Grammie, Grammie!"

As soon as the wolf crossed the threshold, he blew out the candle, saying the light hurt his tired eyes. Felice pulled a chair forward for her grandmother. The wolf sat down hard on his tail hidden under the skirt.

"Ouch!" he exclaimed.

"Is something wrong, Grammie?" asked Felice.

"Nothing at all, my dear," said the wolf, bearing the pain silently.

Then Mayling and Jeanne wanted to sit on their Grammie's lap.

"What nice, plump children," said the wolf, holding Mayling on one knee and Jeanne on the other.

Soon the wolf said, "Grammie is tired and so are you children. Let's go to bed."

The children begged as usual to be allowed to sleep in the huge double bed with their Grammie.

Soon Jeanne felt the wolf's tail against her toes. "Grammie, what's that furry thing?" she asked.

"Oh, that's just the brush I always have by me to keep away mosquitoes and flies," answered the wolf.

Then Mayling felt the sharp claws of the wolf. "Grammie, what are these sharp things?"

"Go to sleep, dear, they are just Grammie's nails."

Then Felice lit the candle and caught a glimpse of the wolf's hairy face before he could blow out the light. Felice was frightened. She quickly grabbed hold of Jeanne and said, "Grammie, Jeanne is thirsty. She needs to get up to get a glass of water."

"Oh, for goodness sake," said the wolf, losing patience, "tell her to wait until later."

Felice pinched Jeanne so that she started to cry.

"All right, all right," said the wolf, "Jeanne may get up."

Felice thought quickly and said, "Mayling, hurry and help Jeanne get a glass of water!"

When the two younger ones had left the bedroom, Felice said, "Grammie, have you ever tasted our luscious gingko nuts?"

"What is a gingko nut?" asked the wolf.

"The meat of the gingko nut is softer and more tender than a firm baby and tastes like a delicious fairy food," replied Felice.

"Where can you get some?" asked the wolf, drooling.

"Those nuts grow on trees outside our house."

"Well, your Grammie is too old to climb trees now," sighed the wolf.

"Grammie, dear, I can pick some for you," said Felice sweetly.

"Will you, angel?" pleaded the wolf.

"Of course, I'll do it right now!" said Felice, leaping out of bed.

"Come back quickly," called the wolf after her.

Felice found Mayling and Jeanne in the other room. She told them about the wolf, and the three girls quickly decided to climb up the tallest gingko tree around their cottage.

The wolf waited and waited, but no one came back. Then he got up and went outside and shouted, "Felice, Mayling, Jeanne, where are you?"

"We're up in the tree, eating gingko nuts," called Felice.

"Throw some down for me," yelled the wolf.

"Ah, Grammie, we just remembered Mummy telling us that gingkos are fairy nuts. They change when they leave the tree. You'll just have to climb up and eat these mouth-watering nuts here."

The wolf was raging as he paced back and forth under the tree.

Then Felice said, "Grammie, I just had an idea. There is a clothes-basket by the door with a long clothes-line inside. Tie one end to the handle and throw the end of the rope up to me. We shall pull you up here."

The wolf happily went to get the clothes-basket.

Felice pulled hard on the rope. When the basket was halfway up, she let go, and the wolf fell to the ground badly bruised.

"Boo hoo, hoo!" cried Felice, pretending to be very sorry. "I did not have enough strength to pull poor Grammie up!"

"Don't cry, Sister," said Mayling, "I'll help you pull Grammie up!"

The greedy wolf got into the basket again.

Felice and Mayling pulled with all their might. The wolf was two-thirds up the tree before they let go of the rope. Down he fell with a crash. He began to scold.

"Grammie, Grammie, please don't get so upset," begged Jeanne. "I'll help my sisters to pull you all the way this time."

"All right, but mind you be very careful or I'll bite your heads off!" screeched the wolf.

The three children pulled with all their strength.

"Heave ho, heave ho!" they sang in rhythm as they hauled the wolf up slowly till he was thirty feet high. He was just beyond reach of a branch when Felice coughed and everyone let go of the rope. As the basket spun down, the wolf let out his last howl.

When the children were unable to get any answer to their calls of "Grammie," they slid down the tree and ran into the house, latched the door and soon went to sleep.

FLOSSIE AND THE FOX[1]

Patricia C. McKissack

Author's Note

Long before I became a writer, I was a listener. On hot summer evenings our family sat on the porch and listened to my grandmother dramatize a Dunbar poem. But it was always a special treat when my grandfather took the stage. He was a master storyteller who charmed his audience with humorous stories told in the rich and colorful dialect of the rural South. I never wanted to forget them. So, it is through me that my family's storytelling legacy lives on.

Here is a story from my youth, retold in the same rich and colorful language that was my grandfather's. He began all his yarns with a question. "Did I ever tell you 'bout the time lil' Flossie Finley come out the Piney Woods heeling a fox?" I'd snuggle up beside him in the big porch swing, then he'd begin his tale...

"Flo-o-o-ossie!"

The sound of Big Mama's voice floated past the cabins in Sophie's Quarters, round the smokehouse, beyond the chicken coop, all the way down to Flossie Finley. Flossie tucked away her straw doll in a hollow log, then hurried to answer her grandmother's call.

"Here I am, Big Mama," Flossie said after catching her breath. It was hot, hotter than a usual Tennessee August day.

---

1   Published in 1986 (New York: Dial).

Big Mama stopped sortin' peaches and wiped her hands and face with her apron. "Take these to Miz Viola over at the McCutchin Place," she say reaching behind her and handing Flossie a basket of fresh eggs. "Seem like they been troubled by a fox. Miz Viola's chickens be so scared, they can't even now lay a stone." Big Mama clicked her teeth and shook her head.

"Why come Mr. J.W. can't catch the fox with his dogs?" Flossie asked, putting a peach in her apron pocket to eat later.

"Ever-time they corner that ol' slickster, he gets away. I tell you, that fox is one sly critter."

"How do a fox look?" Flossie asked. "I disremember ever seeing one."

Big Mama had to think a bit. "Chile, a fox be just a fox. But one thing for sure, that rascal loves eggs. He'll do most anything to get at some eggs."

Flossie tucked the basket under her arm and started on her way. "Don't tarry now," Big Mama called. "And be particular 'bout them eggs."

"Yes'um," Flossie answered.

The way through the woods was shorter and cooler than the road route under the open sun. *What if I come upon a fox?* thought Flossie. *Oh well, a fox be just a fox. That aine so scary.*

Flossie commenced to skip along, when she come upon a critter she couldn't recollect ever seeing. He was sittin' 'side the road like he was expectin' somebody. Flossie skipped right up to him and nodded a greeting the way she'd been taught to do.

"Top of the morning to you, Little Missy," the critter replied. "And what is your name?"

"I be Flossie Finley," she answered with a proper curtsy. "I reckon I don't know who you be either."

Slowly the animal circled round Flossie. "I am a fox," he announced, all the time eyeing the basket of eggs. He stopped in front of Flossie, smiled as best a fox can, and bowed. "At your service."

Flossie rocked back on her heels then up on her toes, back and forward, back and forward … carefully studying the creature who was claiming to be a fox.

"Nope," she said at last. "I just purely don't believe it."

"You don't believe what?" Fox asked, looking way from the basket of eggs for the first time.

"I don't believe you a fox, that's what."

Fox's eyes flashed anger. Then he chuckled softly. "My dear child," he said, sounding right disgusted, "of course I'm a fox. A little girl like you should be simply terrified of me. Whatever do they teach children these days?"

Flossie tossed her head in the air. "Well, whatever you are, you sho' think a heap of yo'self," she said and skipped away.

Fox looked shocked. "Wait," he called. "You mean … you're not frightened? Not just a bit?"

Flossie stopped. Then she turned and say, "I aine never seen a fox before. So, why should I be scared of you and I don't even-now know you a real fox for a fact?"

Fox pulled himself tall. He cleared his throat. "Are you saying I must offer proof that I am a fox before you will be frightened of me?"

"That's just what I'm saying."

Lil' Flossie skipped on through the piney woods while that Fox fella rushed away lookin' for whatever he needed to prove he was really who he said he was.

Meanwhile Flossie stopped to rest 'side a tree. Suddenly Fox was beside her. "I have the proof," he said. "See, I have thick, luxurious fur. Feel for yourself."

Fox leaned over for Flossie to rub his back.

"Ummm. Feels like rabbit fur to me," she say to Fox. "Shucks! You aine no fox. You a rabbit, all the time trying to fool me."

"Me! A rabbit!" he shouted. "I have you know my reputation precedes me. I am the third generation of foxes who have out-smarted and out-run Mr. J.W. Mc-Cutchin's fine hunting dogs. I have raided some of the best henhouses from Franklin to Madison. Rabbit, indeed! I am a fox, and you will act accordingly!"

Flossie hopped to her feet. She put her free hand on her hip and patted her foot. "Unless you can show you a fox, I'll not accord you nothing!" And without further ceremony she skipped away.

Down the road apiece, Flossie stopped by a bubbling spring. She knelt to get a drink of water. Fox came up to her and said, "I have a long pointed nose. Now that should be proof enough."

"Don't prove a thing to me." Flossie picked some wild flowers. "Come to think of it," she said matter-of-fact-like, "rats got long pointed noses." She snapped her fingers. "That's it! You a rat trying to pass yo'self off as a fox."

That near 'bout took Fox's breath away. "I beg your pardon," he gasped.

"You can beg all you wanna," Flossie say skipping on down the road. "That still don't make you no fox."

"I'll teach you a thing or two, young lady," Fox called after her. "You just wait and see."

Before long Flossie came to a clearing. A large orange tabby was sunning on a tree stump. "Hi, pretty kitty," the girl say and rubbed the cat behind her ears. Meanwhile Fox slipped from behind a clump of bushes.

"Since you won't believe me when I tell you I am a fox," he said stiffly, "perhaps you will believe that fine feline creature toward whom you seem to have some measure of respect."

Flossie looked at the cat and winked her eye. "He sho' use a heap of words," she whispered.

Fox beckoned for Cat to speak up. Cat jumped to a nearby log and yawned and stretched—then she answered. "This is a fox because he has sharp claws and yellow eyes," she purred.

Fox seemed satisfied. But Flossie looked at the cat. She looked at Fox, then once more at both just to be sure. She say, "All due respect, Miz Cat, but both y'all got sharp claws and yellow eyes. So … that don't prove nothing, cep'n both y'all be cats."

Fox went to howling and running round in circles. He was plum beside himself. "I am a fox and I know it," he shouted. "This is absurd!"

"No call for you to use that kind of language," Flossie said and she skipped away.

"Wait, wait," Fox followed pleading. "I just remembered something. It may be the solution to this—this horrible situation."

"Good. It's about time."

"I—I—I have a bushy tail." Fox seemed to perk up. "That's right," he said. "All foxes are known for their fluffy, bushy tails. That has got to be adequate proof."

"Aine got to be. You got a bushy tail. So do squirrels." Flossie pointed to one overhead leaping from branch to branch in the tree tops. "Here, have a bite of peach," she said, offering Fox first bite of her treat.

But Fox was crying like a natural born baby. "No, no, no," he sobbed. "If I promise you I'm a fox, won't that do?"

Flossie shook her head no.

"Oh, woe is me," Fox hollered. "I may never recover my confidence."

Flossie didn't stop walking. "That's just what I been saying. You just an ol' confidencer. Come tellin' me you was a fox, then can't prove it. Shame on you!"

Long about that time, Flossie and the fox came out of the woods. Flossie cupped her hands over her eyes and caught sight of McCutchin Quarters and Miz Viola's cabin. Fox didn't notice a thing; he just followed behind Flossie begging to be believed.

"Give me one last chance," he pleaded.

Flossie turned on her heels. "Okay. But just this once more."

Fox tried not to whimper, but his voice was real unsteady-like. "I—I have sharp teeth and I can run exceedingly fast." He waited for Flossie to say something.

Slowly the girl rocked from heel to toe … back and forward. "You know," she finally said, smiling, "it don't make much difference what I think anymore."

"What?" Fox asked. "Why?"

"Cause there's one of Mr. J.W. McCutchin's hounds behind you. He's got sharp teeth and can run fast too. And, by the way that hound's lookin', it's all over for you!"

With a quick glance back Fox dashed toward the woods. "The hound knows who I am!" he shouted. "But I'm not worried. I sure can out-smart and out-run one of Mr. J.W. McCutchin's miserable mutts any old time of the day, because like I told you, I am a fox!"

"I know," said Flossie. "I know." And she turned toward Miz Viola's with the basket of eggs safely tucked under her arm.

LITTLE RED RIDING HOOD[1]

David McPhail

ONCE THERE WAS A GIRL called Little Red Riding Hood because, whenever she went out, she wore a pretty red cape.

One day her mother baked some cookies and asked Little Red Riding Hood to take them to Grandmother, who was ill and could not leave her bed.

"Stay on the path and don't dawdle," instructed Little Red Riding Hood's mother. And the girl started off.

Little Red Riding Hood was about halfway to Grandmother's house when she met a wolf, but as she didn't know what a bad sort of animal he was, she did not feel afraid.

"Where are you off to so early this fine day?" inquired the wolf.

"I'm taking some cookies to my grandmother," answered Little Red Riding Hood.

"And where does your grandmother live?" the wolf persisted.

"Her house stands beneath the three oak trees," said Little Red Riding Hood.

As she was innocently explaining all this, the wolf was thinking, *If I can get there before her, I'll eat the grandmother for my main course and this tender young morsel for my dessert.*

"Your grandmother would surely love a bouquet of flowers," the wolf said to Little Red Riding Hood.

And that set Little Red Riding Hood to thinking about it.

So Little Red Riding Hood ventured farther and farther off the path to pick flowers, while the wolf went hastily to Grandmother's house and knocked on the door.

"Who's there?" called the grandmother in a very weak voice.

---

1   Published in 1995 (New York: Scholastic).

"It's your dear granddaughter," lied the wolf. "Please open the door."

"Come in," said the grandmother. "The door is not locked."

As soon as the door opened, the grandmother realized her mistake.

For instead of the darling Little Red Riding Hood, a wicked wolf stepped into the room. And though the grandmother's body was weak, she ran into the wardrobe and locked the door.

The wolf would have torn the door right off its hinges, but through the window, he saw Little Red Riding Hood walking down the path.

So the wolf put on the grandmother's cap and glasses, which had fallen to the floor, climbed into the bed, and pulled the covers up to his chin.

When she got to her grandmother's house, Little Red Riding Hood was surprised to see an open door. Nevertheless, she stepped inside.

"Good morning, Grandmother," she called. But there was no answer. Little Red Riding Hood stepped closer to the bed.

As the curtain had been drawn around the bed, Little Red Riding Hood could not see clearly in the dim light. "Oh, Grandmother," she exclaimed, "what big *ears* you have!"

"All the better to *hear* you with," said the wolf.

"Oh, Grandmother," said Little Red Riding Hood, "what big *eyes* you have!"

"All the better to *see* you with," said the wolf.

"Oh, Grandmother," said Little Red Riding Hood, "what big *teeth* you have!"

"All the better to *eat* you with!" said the wolf and he threw back the covers.

But Little Red Riding Hood was too quick for the wolf, and before he could catch her, she crawled under the bed.

The angry wolf went after her, but as he was much bigger than Little Red Riding Hood, he got stuck.

Little Red Riding Hood came out from under the bed and jumped on top of it. She jumped up and down, and shouted at the top of her voice, "Help! Help! There's a big bad wolf in here, and I fear he has eaten my grandmother!"

Little Red Riding Hood's grandmother, on hearing this, came out of the wardrobe.

Meanwhile, everyone who happened to be in the forest that day, including a woodcutter with a mighty sharp ax, heard Little Red Riding Hood's cries and ran to help.

They had nearly reached the cottage when the wolf finally managed to squeeze out from under the bed and stagger through the door.

The last time Little Red Riding Hood saw the wolf, he was running down the path, followed closely by a hostile crowd.

And Little Red Riding Hood never saw or heard from him again.

WOLF[1]

Francesca Lia Block

THEY DON'T BELIEVE ME. THEY think I'm crazy. But let me tell you something it be a wicked wicked world out there if you didn't already know.

My mom and he were fighting and that was nothing new. And he was drinking, same old thing. But then I heard her mention me, how she knew what he was doing. And no fucking way was she going to sit around and let that happen. She was taking me away and he better not try to stop her. He said, no way, she couldn't leave.

That's when I started getting scared for both of us, my mom and me. How the hell did she know about that? He would think for sure I told her. And then he'd do what he had promised he'd do every night he held me under the crush of his putrid skanky body.

I knew I had to get out of there. I put all my stuff together as quick and quiet as possible—just some clothes, and this one stuffed lamb my mom gave me when I was little and my piggy-bank money that I'd been saving—and I climbed out the window of the condo. It was a hot night and I could smell my own sweat but it was different. I smelled the same old fear I'm used to but it was mixed with the night and the air and the moon and the trees and it was like freedom, that's what I smelled on my skin.

Same old boring boring story America can't stop telling itself. What is this sicko fascination? Every book and movie practically has to have a little, right? But why do you think all those runaways are on the streets tearing up their veins with junk and selling themselves so they can sleep in the gutter? What do you think the alternative was at home?

I booked because I am not a victim by nature. I had been planning on leaving, but I didn't want to lose my mom and I knew the only way I could get her to leave him was if I told her what he did. That was out of the question, not only because of what he might do to me but what it would do to her.

I knew I had to go back and help her, but I have to admit to you that at that moment I was scared shitless and it didn't seem like the time to try any heroics. That's when I knew I had to get to the desert because there was only one person I had in the world besides my mom.

I really love my mom. You know we were like best friends and I didn't even really need any other friend. She was so much fun to hang with. We cut each other's hair and shared clothes. Her taste was kind of youngish and cute, but it worked because she looked pretty young. People thought we were sisters. She knew all the song

---

1   From *The Rose and the Beast*, 2000 (New York: Harper Collins).

lyrics and we sang along in the car. We both can't carry a tune. Couldn't? What else about her? It's so hard to think of things sometimes, when you're trying to describe somebody so someone else will know. But that's the thing about it—no one can ever know. Basically you're totally alone and the only person in the world who made me feel not completely that way was her because after all we were made of the same stuff. She used to say to me, Baby, I'll always be with you. No matter what happens to me I'm still here. I believed her until he started coming into my room. Maybe she was still with me but I couldn't be with her those times. It was like if I did then she'd hurt so bad I'd lose her forever.

I figured the only place I could go would be to the desert, so I got together all my money and went to the bus station and bought a ticket. On the ride I started getting the shakes real bad thinking that maybe I shouldn't have left my mom alone like that and maybe I should go back but I was chickenshit, I guess. I leaned my head on the glass and it felt cool and when we got out of the city I started feeling a little better like I could breathe. L.A. isn't really so bad as people think. I guess. I mean there are gangs at my school but they aren't really active or violent except for the isolated incident. I have experienced one big earthquake in my life and it really didn't bother me so much because I'd rather feel out of control at the mercy of nature than other ways, if you know what I mean. I just closed my eyes and let it ride itself out. I kind of wished he'd been on top of me then because it might have scared him and made him feel retribution was at hand, but I seriously doubt that. I don't blame the earth for shaking because she is probably so sick of people fucking with her all the time—building things and poisoning her and that. L.A. is also known for the smog, but my mom said that when she was growing up it was way worse and that they had to have smog alerts all the time where they couldn't do P.E.[1] Now that part I would have liked because P.E. sucks. I'm not very athletic, maybe cause I smoke, and I hate getting undressed in front of some of those stupid bitches who like to see what kind of underwear you have on so they can dis you in yet another ingenious way. Anyway, my smoking is way worse for my lungs than the smog, so I don't care about it too much. My mom hated that I smoke and she tried everything—tears and the patch and Nicorette and homeopathic remedies and trips to an acupuncturist, but finally she gave up.

I was wanting a cigarette bad on that bus and thinking about how it would taste, better than the normal taste in my mouth, which I consider tainted by him, and how I can always weirdly breathe a lot better when I have one. My mom read somewhere that smoker's smoke as a way to breathe more, so yoga is supposed to help, but that is one thing she couldn't get me to try. My grandmother, I knew she wouldn't mind the smoking—what could she say? My mom called her Barb the chimney. There

---

1   P.E.: Physical education class.

is something so dry and brittle, so sort of flammable about her, you'd think it'd be dangerous for her to light up like that.

I liked the desert from when I visited there. I liked that it was hot and clean-feeling, and the sand and rocks and cactus didn't make you think too much about love and if you had it or not. They kind of made your mind still, whereas L.A.—even the best parts, maybe especially the best parts, like flowering trees and neon signs and different kinds of ethnic food and music—made you feel agitated and like you were never really getting what you needed. Maybe L.A. had some untapped resources and hidden treasures that would make me feel full and happy and that I didn't know about yet but I wasn't dying to find them just then. If I had a choice I'd probably like to go to Bali or someplace like that where people are more natural and believe in art and dreams and color and love. Does any place like that exist? The main reason L.A. was okay was because that is where my mom was and anywhere she was I had decided to make my home.

On the bus there was this boy with straight brown hair hanging in his pale freckled face. He looked really sad. I wanted to talk to him so much but of course I didn't. I am freaked that if I get close to a boy he will somehow find out what happened to me—like it's a scar he'll see or a smell or something, a red flag—and he'll hate me and go away. This boy kind of looked like maybe something had happened to him, too, but you can't know for sure. Sometimes I'd think I'd see signs of it in people but then I wondered if I was just trying not to feel so alone. That sounds sick, I guess, trying to almost wish what I went through on someone else for company. But I don't mean it that way. I don't wish it on anyone, believe me, but if they've been there I would like to talk to them about it.

The boy was writing furiously in a notebook, like maybe a journal, which I thought was cool. This journal now is the best thing I've ever done in my whole life. It's the only good thing really that they've given me here.

One of our assignments was to write about your perfect dream day. I wonder what this boy's perfect dream day would be. Probably to get to fuck Pamela Lee or something. Unless he was really as cool as I hoped, in which case it would be to wake up in a bed full of cute kitties and puppies and eat a bowl full of chocolate chip cookies in milk and get on a plane and get to go to a warm, clean, safe place (the cats and dogs would arrive there later, not at all stressed from their journey) where you could swim in blue-crystal water all day naked without being afraid and you could lie in the sun and tell your best friend (who was also there) your funniest stories so that you both laughed so hard you thought you'd pop and at night you got to go to a restaurant full of balloons and candles and stuffed bears, like my birthdays when I was little, and eat mounds of ice cream after removing the circuses of tiny plastic animals from on top.

In my case, the best friend would be my mom, of course, and maybe this boy if he turned out to be real cool and not stupid. I fell asleep for a little while and I had this really bad dream. I can't remember what it was but I woke up feeling like someone had been slugging me. And then I thought about my mom, I waited to feel her there with me, like I did whenever I was scared, but it was like those times when he came into my room—she wasn't anywhere. She was gone then and I think that was when I knew but I wouldn't let myself.

I think when you are born an angel should say to you, hopefully kindly and not in the fake voice of an airline attendant: Here you go on this long, long dream. Don't even try to wake up. Just let it go on until it is over. You will learn many things. Just relax and observe because there just is pain and that's it mostly and you aren't going to be able to escape no matter what. Eventually it will all be over anyway. Good luck.

I had to get off the bus before the boy with the notebook and as I passed him he looked up. I saw in his journal that he hadn't been writing but sketching, and he ripped out a page and handed it to me. I saw it was a picture of a girl's face but that is all that registered because I was thinking about how my stomach had dropped, how I had to keep walking, step by step, and get off the bus and I'd never be able to see him again and somehow it really really mattered.

When I got off the bus and lit up I saw that the picture was me—except way prettier than I think I look, but just as sad as I feel. And then it was too late to do anything because the bus was gone and so was he.

I stopped at the liquor store and bought a bag of pretzels and a Mountain Dew because I hadn't eaten all day and my stomach was talking pretty loud. Everything tasted of bitter smoke. Then after I'd eaten I started walking along the road to my grandma's. She lives off the highway on this dirt road surrounded by cactus and other desert plants. It was pretty dark so you could see the stars really big and bright, and I thought how cold the sky was and not welcoming or magical at all. It just made me feel really lonely. A bat flew past like a sharp shadow and I could hear owls and coyotes. The coyote howls were the sound I would have made if I could have. Deep and sad but scary enough that no one would mess with me, either.

My grandma has a used stuff store so her house is like this crazy warehouse full of junk like those little plaster statuettes from the seventies of these ugly little kids with stupid sayings that are supposed to be funny, and lots of old clothes like army jackets and jeans and ladies' nylon shirts, and cocktail glasses, broken china, old books, trinkets, gadgets, just a lot of stuff that you think no one would want but they do, I guess, because she's been in business a long time. Mostly people come just to talk to her because she is sort of this wise woman of the desert who's been through a lot in her life and then they end up buying something, I think, as a way to pay her back for the free counseling. She's cool, with a desert-lined face and a bandanna over her hair and long skinny legs in jeans. She was always after my mom to drop that guy and move out here with her but my mom wouldn't. My mom still was holding on to her secret dream of being an actress but nothing had panned out yet. She was so pretty, I thought it would, though. Even though she had started to look a little older. But she could have gotten those commercials where they use the women her age to sell household products and aspirin and stuff. She would have been good at that because of her face and her voice, which are kind and honest and you just trust her.

I hadn't told Grandma anything about him, but I think she knew that he was fucked up. She didn't know how much, though, or she wouldn't have let us stay there. Sometimes I wanted to go and tell her, but I was afraid then Mom would have to know and maybe hate me so much that she'd kick me out.

My mom and I used to get dressed up and put makeup on each other and pretend to do commercials. We had this mother-daughter one that was pretty cool. She said I was a natural, but I wouldn't want to be an actor because I didn't like people looking at me that much. Except that boy on the bus, because his drawing wasn't about the outside of my body, but how I felt inside and you could tell by the way he did it, and the way he smiled, that he understood those feelings so I didn't mind that he saw them. My mom felt that I'd be good anyway, because she said that a lot of actors don't like people looking at them and that is how they create these personas to hide behind so people will see that and the really good ones are created to hide a lot of things. I guess for that reason I might be okay but I still hated the idea of going on auditions and having people tell me I wasn't pretty enough or something. My mom said it was interesting and challenging but I saw it start to wear on her.

Grandma wasn't there when I knocked so I went around the back, where she sat sometimes at night to smoke, and it was quiet there, too. That's when I started feeling sick like at night in my bed trying not to breathe or vomit. Because I saw his Buick sitting there in the sand.

Maybe I have read too many fairy tales. Maybe no one will believe me.

I poked around the house and looked through the windows and after a while I heard their voices and I saw them in this cluttered little storage room piled up with the stuff she sells at the store. Everything looked this glazed brown fluorescent color. When I saw his face I knew something really bad had happened. I remembered the dream I had had and thought about my mom. All of a sudden I was inside that room, I don't really remember how I got there, but I was standing next to my grandma and I saw she had her shotgun in her hand.

He was saying, Barb, calm down, now, okay. Just calm down. When he saw me his eyes narrowed like dark slashes and I heard a coyote out in the night.

My grandmother looked at me and at him and her mouth was this little line stitched up with wrinkles. She kept looking at him but she said to me, Babe, are you okay?

I said I had heard him yelling at mom and I left. She asked him what happened with Nance and he said they had a little argument, that was all, put down the gun, please, Barb.

Then I just lost it, I saw my grandma maybe start to back down a little and I went ballistic. I started screaming how he had raped me for years and I wanted to kill him and if we didn't he'd kill us. Maybe my mom was already dead.

I don't know what else I said, but I do know that he started laughing at me, this hideous tooth laugh, and I remembered him above me in that bed with his clammy hand on my mouth and his ugly ugly weight and me trying to keep hanging on because I wouldn't let him take my mom away, that was the one thing he could never do and now he had. Then I had the gun and I pulled the trigger. My grandma had taught me how once, without my mom knowing, in case I ever needed to defend myself, she said.

My grandma says that she did it. She says that he came at us and she said to him, I've killed a lot prettier, sweeter innocents than you with this shotgun, meaning the animals when she used to go out hunting, which is a pretty good line and everything, but she didn't do it. It was me.

I have no regrets about him. I don't care about much anymore, really. Only one thing.

Maybe one night I'll be asleep and I'll feel a hand like a dove on my cheekbone and feel her breath cool like peppermints and when I open my eyes my mom will be there like an angel, saying in the softest voice, When you are born it is like a long, long dream. Don't try to wake up. Just go along until it is over. Don't be afraid. You may not know it all the time but I am with you. I am with you.

SLEEPING BEAUTY

Few fairy tales have achieved greater popularity—or provoked more controversy—than "Sleeping Beauty." The hundred-year enchanted sleep endured by the central character is at the same time a memorable narrative ploy and a vivid symbol of feminine passivity; it is no wonder, therefore, that feminist critics have seen a darker aspect to the tale's continued success.

As in the previous section, there can be little doubt that the earlier version (or versions) had a definite influence upon its successors—but in this case, the result of that influence is clearly different. In the versions of "Little Red Riding Hood," we can see the process of literary refinement in the tale's elaboration; now that same process takes the opposite tack, as the tale undergoes significant shrinkage (particularly between Perrault and the Grimms) in the effort to make the tale suitable for its ever-younger audience.

Despite the obvious differences between these versions, the central image of the enchanted sleep remains constant and is arguably the key to the popularity of the tale. So the question arises: how could an image of extended inactivity be so crucial to the tale's success? One answer, as P.L. Travers points out in an insightful essay on this tale,[1] is that the central image of a sleeping princess awaiting the prince who will

---

1   P.L. Travers, *About the Sleeping Beauty* (New York: McGraw-Hill, 1975) 47-62. Travers takes pains to remind us of the multi-faceted nature of the symbol, which she illustrates most effectively in a list of famous sleepers whose concerns often have little to do with growing up: "The idea of the sleeper, of somebody hidden from mortal eye, waiting until the time shall ripen has always been dear to the folkly mind—Snow White asleep in her glass coffin, Brynhild behind her wall of fire, Charlemagne in the heart of France, King Arthur in the Isle of Avalon, Frederick Barbarossa under his mountain in Thuringia. Muchukunda, the Hindu King, slept through eons till he was awakened by the Lord Krishna; Oisin of Ireland dreamed in Tir n'an Og for over three hundred years. Psyche in her magic sleep is a type of Sleeping Beauty, Sumerian Ishtar in the underworld may be said to be another. Holga the Dane is sleeping and waiting, and so, they say, is Sir Francis Drake. Quetzalcoatl of Mexico and Virochocha of Peru are both sleepers. Morgan le Fay of France and England and Dame Holle of Germany are sleeping in raths and cairns" (51).

bring her (and her whole world) back to life has powerful mythic overtones of death and resurrection. On a more human level, the image is a metaphor of growing up: in each case the heroine falls asleep as a naive girl and awakens as a mature young woman on the threshold of marriage and adult responsibility. For cultural reasons, the metaphor is generally seen as gender-specific, in that sleep denotes the decorous passivity expected of the virtuous young female—a characteristic that undoubtedly attracted nineteenth-century approval of this tale. By contrast, the young male must demonstrate his maturity through deeds of daring, manifested most effectively in Perrault's version of the tale.

Giambattista Basile (1575-1632) was a minor Neapolitan courtier and soldier who was among the first in the Western world to commit the folk tale to paper. It becomes quickly apparent, however, that Basile's tales in *The Pentamerone* (1634) are a good deal more sophisticated than we expect a fairy tale to be; their content, tone, and overall structure hearken back to Boccaccio and Chaucer rather than anticipate the fairy-tale collections that would follow. This quality is well illustrated by Basile's version of "Sleeping Beauty," which is a story of rape, adultery, sexual rivalry, and attempted cannibalism—a far cry from what we have come to expect in this famous tale!

Comparing Basile's tale with Perrault's "Sleeping Beauty in the Wood" provides a fascinating glimpse into the evolution of a tale in its literary form, as the Frenchman sets about revising it to match *his* assumptions about what a fairy tale is and who will read (or hear) it. In a nutshell, it might be said that Perrault's approach is rather more subtle than that of his Neapolitan predecessor. Clearly, Perrault wants no part of Basile's evident delight in the salacious aspects of his story. While as a royal courtier he was doubtless no stranger to confrontations between jealous wives and beautiful mistresses, his tale suggests that discretion and a sophisticated cynicism are now the rule in dealing with such matters; social diplomat that he is, Perrault favors the oblique comment, the aside that demonstrates the wit of the writer and makes an accomplice of the reader. Thus Perrault's prince refrains—at least at the moment of discovery—from all physical contact with the sleeping princess (he is simply present when the enchantment reaches full term, whereas the spell-breaking kiss bestowed by the Grimms' prince implies an arousal that is sexual in nature). We may detect more than a trace of archness, however, when Perrault tells us that the young couple "... did not sleep much, that night; the princess did not feel in the least drowsy." Likewise, through his use of symbolism, Perrault finds a way to sublimate the sexual rivalry that gives Basile's more realistic tale much of its impact. In Perrault's version, the King's tigerish wife becomes the Prince's ogress mother, which allows the retention of several significant elements (such as the cannibalism motif), while further deflecting the violence of the tale with a characteristic touch of sly humor: her intention to eat one of Sleeping Beauty's children is horrific, of course—but there is a certain Gallic *savoir-faire* in the instruction to her steward to "… serve her up with sauce Robert." To modern eyes, Perrault's alteration of the tale clearly invites a Freudian interpretation, as the Prince's mother wages her ruthless campaign to destroy all rivals for her son's affections. As suggested above, the lesser-known sequel contains an intriguing insight into *male* maturation, counterpointing Sleeping Beauty's transformation by sleep. The crisis of this episode is brought on by the prince's assumption that becoming king is the external confirmation of his personal maturity; he therefore chooses this moment to reveal the existence of his wife and children to his mother. "Some time afterwards," we are told, in an apparent *non-sequitur* that speaks volumes, "the king decided to declare war on his neighbour, the Emperor Cantalabutte"! Given the prince's awareness of his mother's appetites, how are we to explain such a decision? Is his departure an indication of his naivety, in that he has no inkling of the rivalry that he leaves behind him—or is he in fact so aware of it that he reckons there's more peace to be found in the middle of a battlefield?

After all the excitement of the two earlier versions, it comes as something of a surprise to realize that the much shorter, blander version by the Brothers Grimm is by far the best-known—perhaps for the very reason that the Grimms chose not to darken the blue sky of romance with the storm-clouds of jealousy and sexual rivalry that may loom up in human relationships (although as we noted above, theirs is the version in which Sleeping Beauty's awakening has the clearest sexual connotation). Yet only a moment's thought is necessary to appreciate why they may have made the editorial decision to end the story there; once again, the central importance of the intended audience asserts itself. Perrault's claims notwithstanding, it was only with the Grimms that the fairy tale unequivocally entered the child's domain—and the Grimms took their responsibility seriously. Consequently, no trace of Basile's hand remains, and little enough of Perrault's either: a comparison of the gifts presented to Sleeping Beauty by the fairies in the Perrault and Grimm versions offers an intriguing insight into the different worlds from which these tales come. At the same time, it might be said that in Grimm we see the tale stripped down to its narrative core, revealing most clearly its *oral* origins.

"The Neapolitan Soldier," a tale from Italo Calvino's collection *Italian Folktales* (1956), brings a sturdily proletarian flavor to this otherwise aristocratic tale. The competitive antics of the three soldiers remind us of the more common three-brother motif, in which the smallest (and youngest?) is invariably the hero. Calvino (1923-85), like the Grimms before him, has "improved" the tale a little; he states in his Note that "The original shows the first two soldiers deriding the third because he is from Naples. I made these two Roman and Florentine respectively, to accentu-ate the spirit of the barracks" (736). And although royalty is indeed present in this version, their strategy for discovering the phantom lover—initiated by the princess herself—suggests a particularly egalitarian kind of rule.

Yet the story of Sleeping Beauty is by no means limited to the Western tradition. From the large and somewhat amorphous collection known as the *Arabian Nights* comes "The 9th Captain's Tale," which contains a number of surprises in terms of what it reveals about the evolution of this tale. (Individual tales within the *Arabian Nights* differ considerably in age, but all were recorded long before the publication, in 1550, of the earliest Western fairy-tale collection, *The Facetious Nights*, by Straparola.) For instance, this version offers us a much fuller depiction of the prince—and a much closer look at the nature of his relationship with the girl. Exotic and mysterious though it may seem at first glance, this tale—like so many others, from East or West—is about growing up. In this regard, it bears some resemblance to Perrault's "Sleeping Beauty in the Wood" in its insistence that a relationship cannot work unless both partners have achieved a level of maturity and understanding. In effect, both must go through a ritual death and rebirth (as occurs in initiation rites in traditional societies) to be ready for the responsibilities of an adult relationship.

SUN, MOON, AND TALIA (SOLE, LUNA, E TALIA)[1]

Giambattista Basile

THERE WAS ONCE A GREAT king who, on the birth of his daughter—to whom he gave the name of Talia—commanded all the wise men and seers in the kingdom to come and tell him what her future would be. These wise men, after many consultations, came to the conclusion that she would be exposed to great danger from a small splinter in some flax. Thereupon the King, to prevent any unfortunate accident, commanded that no flax or hemp or any other similar material should ever come into his house.

One day when Talia was grown up she was standing by the window, and saw an old woman pass who was spinning. Talia had never seen a distaff and spindle, and was therefore delighted with the dancing of the spindle. Prompted by curiosity, she had the old woman brought up to her, and taking the distaff in her hand, began to draw out the thread; but unfortunately a splinter in the hemp got under her fingernail, and she immediately fell dead upon the ground. At this terrible catastrophe the

---

1   First published in 1634-36. This text from *The Pentamerone*, trans. Benedetto Croce, ed. N.M. Penzer (London: John Lane, the Bodley Head, 1932).

old woman fled from the room, rushing precipitously down the stairs. The stricken father, after having paid for this bucketful of sour wine with a barrelful of tears, left the dead Talia seated on a velvet chair under an embroidered canopy in the palace, which was in the middle of a wood. Then he locked the door and left forever the house which had brought him such evil fortune, so that he might entirely obliterate the memory of his sorrow and suffering.

It happened some time after that a falcon of a king who was out hunting in these parts flew in at the window of this house. As the bird did not return when called back, the King sent someone to knock at the door, thinking the house was inhabited. When they had knocked a long time in vain, the King sent for a vine-dresser's ladder, so that he might climb up himself and see what was inside. He climbed up and went in, and was astonished at not finding a living being anywhere. Finally he came to the room in which sat Talia as if under a spell.

The King called to her, thinking she was asleep; but since nothing he did or said brought her back to her senses, and being on fire with love, he carried her to a couch and, having gathered the fruits of love, left her lying there. Then he returned to his own kingdom and for a long time entirely forgot the affair.

Nine months later, Talia gave birth to two children, a boy and a girl, two splendid pearls. They were looked after by two fairies, who had appeared in the palace, and who put the babies to their mother's breast. Once, when one of the babies wanted to suck, it could not find the breast, but got into its mouth instead the finger that had been pricked. This the baby sucked so hard that it drew out the splinter, and Talia was roused as if from a deep sleep. When she saw the two jewels at her side, she clasped them to her breast and held them as dear as life; but she could not understand what had happened, and how she came to be alone in the palace with two children, having everything she required to eat brought to her without seeing anyone.

One day the King bethought himself of the adventure of the fair sleeper and took the opportunity of another hunting expedition to go and see her. Finding her awake and with two prodigies of beauty, he was overpowered with joy. He told Talia what had happened and they made a great compact of friendship, and he remained several days in her company. Then he left her, promising to come again and take her back with him to his kingdom. When he reached his home he was forever talking of Talia and her children. At meals the names of Talia, Sun, and Moon (these were the children's names) were always on his lips; when he went to bed he was always calling one or the other.

The Queen had already had some glimmering of suspicion on account of her husband's long absence when hunting; and hearing his continued calling on Talia, Sun, and Moon, burned with a heat very different from the sun's heat, and calling the

King's secretary, said to him: "Listen, my son, you are between Scylla and Charybdis,[1] between the doorpost and the door, between the poker and the grate. If you tell me with whom it is that my husband is in love, I will make you rich; if you hide the truth from me, you shall never be found again, dead or alive." The man, on the one hand moved by fear, and on the other egged on by interest, which is a bandage over the eyes of honour, a blinding of justice and a cast horseshoe to faith, told the Queen all, calling bread bread and wine wine.

Then she sent the same secretary in the King's name to tell Talia that he wished to see his children. Talia was delighted and sent the children. But the Queen, as soon as she had possession of them, with the heart of a Medea,[2] ordered the cook to cut their throats and to make them into hashes and sauces and give them to their unfortunate father to eat.

The cook, who was tender-hearted, was filled with pity on seeing these two golden apples of beauty, and gave them to his wife to hide and prepared two kids,[3] making a hundred different dishes of them. When the hour for dinner arrived, the Queen had the dishes brought in, and whilst the King was eating and enjoying them, exclaiming: "How good this is, by the life of Lanfusa! How tasty this is, by the soul of my grandmother!" she kept encouraging him, saying: "Eat away, you are eating what is your own." The first two or three times the King paid no attention to these words, but as she kept up the same strain of music, he answered: "I know very well I am eating what is my own; you never brought anything into the house." And getting up in a rage, he went off to a villa not far away to cool his anger down.

The Queen, not satisfied with what she thought she had already done, called the secretary again, and sent him to fetch Talia herself, pretending that the King was expecting her. Talia came at once, longing to see the light of her eyes and little guessing that it was fire that awaited her. She was brought before the Queen, who, with the face of a Nero[4] all inflamed with rage, said to her: "Welcome, Madame Troccola![5] So you are the fine piece of goods, the fine flower my husband is enjoying! You are the cursed bitch that makes my head go round! Now you have got into purgatory, and I will make you pay for all the harm you have done me!"

Talia began to excuse herself, saying it was not her fault and that the King had taken possession of her territory whilst she was sleeping. But the Queen would not

---

1   Scylla and Charybdis: Two monsters of Greek mythology who lived on opposite sides of a narrow channel of water. The phrase "between Scylla and Charybdis" means having to choose between two undesirable situations.
2   Medea: One of the great sorceresses in Greek mythology; when her husband left her, she ate their children.
3   Kid: Young goat.
4   Nero: A Roman emperor infamous for his cruelty.
5   Troccola: Busybody.

listen to her, and commanded that a great fire should be lit in the courtyard of the palace and that Talia should be thrown into it.

The unfortunate Talia, seeing herself lost, threw herself on her knees before the Queen, and begged that at least she should be given time to take off the clothes she was wearing. The Queen, not out of pity for her, but because she wanted to save the clothes, which were embroidered with gold and pearls, said: "Undress—that I agree to."

Talia began to undress, and for each garment that she took off she uttered a shriek. She had taken off her dress, her skirt, and bodice and was about to take off her petticoat, and to utter her last cry, and they were just going to drag her away to reduce her to lye ashes, which they would throw into boiling water to wash Charon's[1] breeches with, when the King saw the spectacle and rushed up to learn what was happening. He asked for his children, and heard from his wife, who reproached him for his betrayal of her, how she had made him eat them himself.

The King abandoned himself to despair. "What!" he cried, "am I the wolf of my own sheep? Alas, why did my veins not recognise the fountain of their own blood? You renegade Turk, this barbarous deed is the work of your hands? Go, you shall get what you deserve; there will be no need to send such a tyrant-faced one to the Colosseum to do penance!"

So saying, he ordered that the Queen should be thrown into the fire lighted for Talia, and that the secretary should be thrown in, too, for he had been her handle in this cruel game and the weaver of this wicked web. He would have had the same done to the cook who, as he thought, had cut up his children; but the cook threw himself at the King's feet, saying: "Indeed, my lord, for such a service there should be no other reward than a burning furnace; no pension but a spike-thrust from behind; no entertainment but that of being twisted and shrivelled in the fire; neither could there be any greater honour than for me, a cook, to have my ashes mingle with those of a queen. But this is not the thanks I expect for having saved your children from that spiteful dog who wished to kill them and return to your body what came from it."

The King was beside himself when he heard these words; it seemed to him as if he must be dreaming and that he could not believe his ears. Turning to the cook, he said: "If it is true that you have saved my children, you may be sure I will not leave you turning spits in the kitchen. You shall be in the kitchen of my heart, turning my will just as you please, and you shall have such rewards that you will account yourself the luckiest man in the world."

Whilst the King was speaking, the cook's wife, seeing her husband's difficulties, brought Sun and Moon up to their father, who, playing at the game of three with his wife and children, made a ring of kisses, kissing first one and then the other. He gave

---

1   Charon: The ferryman who rowed the souls of the dead across the river Styx to Hades.

a handsome reward to the cook and made him Gentleman of the Bed-chamber. Talia became his wife, and enjoyed a long life with her husband and children, finding it to be true that:

Lucky people, so 'tis said,
Are blessed by Fortune whilst in bed.

THE SLEEPING BEAUTY IN THE WOOD[1]

Charles Perrault

ONCE UPON A TIME, THERE lived a king and a queen who were bitterly unhappy because they did not have any children. They visited all the clinics, all the specialists, made holy vows, went on pilgrimages and said their prayers regularly but with so little success that when, at long last, the queen finally did conceive and, in due course, gave birth to a daughter, they were both wild with joy. Obviously, this baby's christening must be the grandest of all possible christenings; for her godmothers, she would have as many fairies as they could find in the entire kingdom. According to the custom of those times, each fairy would make the child a magic present, so that the princess could acquire every possible perfection. After a long search, they managed to trace seven suitable fairies.

After the ceremony at the church, the guests went back to the royal palace for a party in honour of the fairy godmothers. Each of these important guests found her place was specially laid with a great dish of gold and a golden knife, fork and spoon studded with diamonds and rubies. But as the fairies took their seats, an uninvited guest came storming into the palace, deeply affronted because she had been forgotten—though it was no wonder she'd been overlooked; this old fairy had hidden herself away in her tower for fifteen years and, since nobody had set eyes on her all that time, they thought she was dead, or had been bewitched. The king ordered a place to be laid for her at once but he could not give her a great gold dish and gold cutlery like the other fairies had because only seven sets had been made. The old fairy was very annoyed at that and muttered threats between her teeth. The fairy who sat beside her overheard her and suspected she planned to revenge herself by giving the little princess a very unpleasant present when the time for present giving came. She

---

1   First published in 1697. This text from *Sleeping Beauty and Other Favourite Fairy Tales,* trans. Angela Carter (London: Gollancz, 1982).

slipped away behind the tapestry so that she could have the last word, if necessary, and put right any harm the old witch might do the baby.

Now the fairies presented their gifts. The youngest fairy said the princess would grow up to be the loveliest woman in the world. The next said she would have the disposition of an angel, the third that she would be graceful as a gazelle, the fourth gave her the gift of dancing, the fifth of singing like a nightingale, and the sixth said she would be able to play any kind of musical instrument that she wanted to.

But when it came to the old fairy's turn, she shook with spite and announced that, in spite of her beauty and accomplishments, the princess was going to prick her finger with a spindle and die of it.

All the guests trembled and wept. But the youngest fairy stepped out from behind the tapestry and cried out:

"Don't despair, King and Queen; your daughter will not die—although, alas, I cannot undo entirely the magic of a senior-ranking fairy. The princess *will* prick her finger with a spindle but, instead of dying, she will fall into a deep sleep that will last for a hundred years. And at the end of a hundred years, the son of a king will come to wake her."

In spite of this comfort, the king did all he could to escape the curse; he forbade the use of a spindle, or even the possession of one, on pain of death, in all the lands he governed.

Fifteen or sixteen years went by. The king and queen were spending the summer at a castle in the country and one day the princess decided to explore, prowling through room after room until at last she climbed up a spiral staircase in a tower and came to an attic in which an old lady was sitting, along with her distaff, spinning, for this old lady had not heard how the king had banned the use of a spindle.

"Whatever are you doing, my good woman?" asked the princess.

"I'm spinning, my dear," answered the old lady.

"Oh, how clever!" said the princess. "How do you do it? Give it to me so that I can see if I can do it, too!"

She was very lively and just a little careless; but besides, and most importantly, the fairies had ordained it. No sooner had she picked up the spindle than she pierced her hand with it and fell down in a faint.

The old lady cried for help and the servants came running from all directions. They threw water over her, unlaced her corsets, slapped her hands, rubbed her temples with *eau-de-cologne*—but nothing would wake her.

The king climbed to the attic to see the cause of the clamour and, sad at heart, knew the fairy's curse had come true. He knew the princess' time had come, just as the fairies said it would, and ordered her to be carried to the finest room in the palace and laid there on a bed covered with gold and silver embroidery. She was as beautiful as an angel. Her trance had not yet taken the colour from her face; her cheeks were rosy and her lips like coral. Her eyes were closed but you could hear her breathing very, very softly and, if you saw the slow movement of her breast, you knew she was not dead.

The king ordered she should be left in peace until the time came when she would wake up. At the moment the princess had pricked her finger, the good fairy who saved her life was in the realm of Mataquin, twelve thousand leagues away, but she heard the news immediately from a dwarf who sped to her in a pair of seven-league boots. The fairy left Mataquin at once in a fiery chariot drawn by dragons and arrived at the grieving court an hour later. The king went out to help her down; she approved of all his arrangements but she was very sensitive, and she thought how sad the princess would be when she woke up all alone in that great castle.

So she touched everything in the house, except for the king and queen, with her magic ring—the housekeepers, the maids of honour, the chambermaids, the gentlemen-in-waiting, the court officials, the cooks, the scullions, the errand-boys, the night-watchmen, the Swiss guards, the page-boys, the footmen; she touched all the horses in the stable, and the stable-boys, too, and even Puff, the princess' little lap-dog, who was curled up on her bed beside her. As soon as she touched them with her magic ring, they all fell fast asleep and would not wake up until their mistress woke, ready to look after her when she needed them. Even the spits on the fire, loaded with partridges and pheasants, drowsed off to sleep, and the flames died down and slept, too. All this took only a moment; fairies are fast workers.

The king and queen kissed their darling child but she did not stir. Then they left the palace forever and issued proclamations forbidding anyone to approach it. Within a quarter of an hour, a great number of trees, some large, some small, interlaced with brambles and thorns, sprang up around the park and formed a hedge so thick that neither man nor beast could penetrate it. This hedge grew so tall that you could see only the topmost turrets of the castle, for the fairy had made a safe, magic place where the princess could sleep her sleep out free from prying eyes.

At the end of a hundred years, the son of the king who now ruled over the country went out hunting in that region. He asked the local people what those turrets he could see above the great wood might mean. They replied, each one, as he had heard tell—how it was an old ruin, full of ghosts; or, that all the witches of the country went there to hold their sabbaths. But the most popular story was, that it was the home of an ogre who carried all the children he caught there, to eat them at his leisure, knowing nobody else could follow him through the wood. The prince did not know what to believe. Then an old man said to him:

"My lord, fifty years ago I heard my father say that the most beautiful princess in all the world was sleeping in that castle, and her sleep was going to last for a hundred years, until the prince who is meant to have her comes to wake her up."

When he heard that, the young prince was tremendously excited; he had never heard of such a marvelous adventure and, fired with thoughts of love and glory, he made up his mind there and then to go through the wood. No sooner had he stepped among the trees than the great trunks and branches, the thorns and brambles parted, to let him pass. He saw the castle at the end of a great avenue and walked towards it, though he was surprised to see that none of his attendants could follow him because the trees sprang together again as soon as he had gone between them. But he did not abandon his quest. A young prince in love is always brave. Then he arrived at a courtyard that seemed like a place where only fear lived.

An awful silence filled it and the look of death was on everything. Man and beast stretched on the ground, like corpses; but the pimples on the red noses of the Swiss guards soon showed him they were not dead at all, but sleeping, and the glasses beside them, with the dregs of wine still at the bottoms, showed how they had dozed off after a spree.

He went through a marble courtyard; he climbed a staircase; he went into a guardroom, where the guards were lined up in two ranks, each with a gun on his shoulder, and snoring with all their might. He found several rooms full of gentlemen-in-waiting and fine ladies; some stood, some sat, all slept. At last he arrived in a room that was entirely covered in gilding and, there on a bed with the curtains drawn back so that he could see her clearly, lay a princess about fifteen or sixteen years old and she was so lovely that she seemed, almost, to shine. The prince approached her trembling, and fell on his knees before her.

The enchantment was over; the princess woke. She gazed at him so tenderly you would not have thought it was the first time she had ever seen him.

"Is it you, my prince?" she said. "You have kept me waiting for a long time."

The prince was beside himself with joy when he heard that and the tenderness in her voice overwhelmed him so that he hardly knew how to reply. He told her he loved her better than he loved himself and though he stumbled over the words, that made her very happy, because he showed so much feeling. He was more tongue-tied than she, because she had had plenty of time to dream of what she would say to him; her good fairy had made sure she had sweet dreams during her long sleep. They talked for hours and still had not said half the things they wanted to say to one another.

But the entire palace had woken up with the princess and everyone was going about his business again. Since none of them were in love, they were all dying of hunger. The chief lady-in-waiting, just as ravenous as the rest, lost patience after a while and told the princess loud and clear that dinner was ready. The prince helped the princess up from the bed and she dressed herself with the greatest magnificence; but when she put on her ruff, the prince remembered how his grandmother had worn one just like it. All the princess' clothes were a hundred years out of fashion, but she was no less beautiful because of that.

Supper was served in the hall of mirrors, while the court orchestra played old tunes on violins and oboes they had not touched for a hundred years. After supper, the chaplain married them in the castle chapel and the chief lady-in-waiting drew the curtains round their bed for them. They did not sleep much, that night; the princess did not feel in the least drowsy. The prince left her in the morning, to return to his father's palace.

The king was anxious because his son had been away so long. The prince told him that he had lost himself in the forest while he was out hunting and had spent the night in a charcoal burner's hut, where his host had given him black bread and cheese to eat. The king believed the story but the queen, the prince's mother, was not so easily hoodwinked when she saw that now the young man spent most of his time out hunting in the forest. Though he always arrived back with an excellent excuse when he had spent two or three nights away from home, his mother soon guessed he was in love.

He lived with the princess for more than two years and he gave her two children. They named the eldest, a daughter, Dawn, because she was so beautiful, but they called their son Day because he came after Dawn and was even more beautiful still.

The queen tried to persuade her son to tell her his secret but he dared not confide in her. Although he loved her, he feared her, because she came from a family of ogres and his father had married her only because she was very, very rich. The court whispered that the queen still had ogrish tastes and could hardly keep her hands off little children, so the prince thought it best to say nothing about his own babies.

But when the king died and the prince himself became king, he felt confident enough to publicly announce his marriage and install the new queen, his wife, in his royal palace with a great deal of ceremony. And soon after that, the new king decided to declare war on his neighbour, the Emperor Cantalabutte.

He left the governing of his kingdom in his mother's hands and he trusted her to look after his wife and children for him, too, because he would be away at war for the whole summer.

As soon as he was gone, the queen mother sent her daughter-in-law and her grandchildren away to the country, to a house deep in the woods, so that she could satisfy her hideous appetites with the greatest of ease. She herself arrived at the house a few days later and said to the butler:

"I want to eat little Dawn for my dinner tomorrow."

"Oh my lady!" exclaimed the butler.

"She's just the very thing I fancy," said the queen mother in the voice of an ogress famished for fresh meat. "And I want you to serve her up with sauce Robert."

The poor man saw he could not argue with a hungry ogress, picked up a carving knife and went to little Dawn's room. She was just four years old. When she saw her dear friend, the butler, she ran up to him, laughing, threw her arms around his neck and asked him where her sweeties were. He burst into tears and the knife fell from his hands. He went down to the farmyard and slaughtered a little lamb instead. He served the lamb up in such a delicious sauce the queen mother said she had never eaten so well in her life and he spirited little Dawn away from harm; he handed her over to his wife, who hid her in a cellar, in the servants' quarters.

Eight days passed. Then the ogress said to the butler:

"I want to eat little Day for my supper."

The butler was determined to outwit her again. He found little Day playing at fencing with his pet monkey; the child was only three. He took him to his wife, who hid him away with his sister, and served up a tender young kid[1] in his place. The queen mother smacked her lips over the dish, so all went well until the night the wicked ogress said to the butler:

"I want to eat the queen with the same sauce you made for her children."

This time, the poor butler did not know what to do. The queen was twenty, now, if you did not count the hundred years she had been asleep; her skin was white and lovely but it was a little tough, and where in all the farmyard was he to find a beast with skin just like it? There was nothing for it; he must kill the queen to save himself and he went to her room, determined he would not have to enter it a second time. He rushed in with a dagger in his hand and told her her mother-in-law had ordered her to die.

"Be quick about it," she said calmly. "Do as she told you. When I am dead, I shall be with my poor children again, my children whom I love so much."

Because they had been taken away from her without a word of explanation, she thought they were dead.

The butler's heart melted.

"No, no, my lady, you don't need to die so that you can be with your children. I've hidden them away from the queen mother's hunger and I will trick her again, I will give her a young deer for supper instead of you."

He took her to the cellar, where he left her kissing her children and weeping over them, and went to kill a young doe that the queen mother ate for supper with as much relish as if it had been her daughter-in-law. She was very pleased with her own cruelty and practiced telling her son how the wolves had eaten his wife and children while he had been away at the wars.

One night as she prowled about as usual, sniffing for the spoor of fresh meat, she heard a voice coming from the servants' quarters. It was little Day's voice; he was

---

1   Kid: Young goat (see p. 51).

crying because he had been naughty and his mother wanted to whip him. Then the queen mother heard Dawn begging her mother to forgive the little boy. The ogress recognised the voices of her grandchildren and she was furious. She ordered a huge vat to be brought into the middle of the courtyard. She had the vat filled with toads, vipers, snakes and serpents and then the queen, her children, the butler, his wife and his maid were brought in front of her with their hands tied behind their backs. She was going to have them thrown into the vat.

The executioners were just on the point of carrying out their dreadful instructions when the king galloped into the courtyard. Nobody had expected him back so soon. He was astonished at what he saw and asked who had commanded the vat and the bonds. The ogress was so angry to see her plans go awry that she jumped head-first into the vat and the vile beasts inside devoured her in an instant. The king could not help grieving a little; after all, she was his mother. But his beautiful wife and children soon made him happy again.

Moral
A brave, rich, handsome husband is a prize well worth waiting for; but no modern woman would think it was worth waiting for a hundred years. The tale of the Sleeping Beauty shows how long engagements make for happy marriages, but young girls these days want so much to be married I do not have the heart to press the moral.

BRIER ROSE[1]
Jacob and Wilhelm Grimm

LONG, LONG AGO THERE LIVED a king and a queen, who said day after day: "Ah, if only we had a child!" but none ever came. Then one day when the queen was sitting in her bath a frog crawled out of the water and said to her: "You will get your wish; before a year goes by, you will bring a daughter into the world." The frog's prediction came true. The queen gave birth to a baby girl who was so beautiful that the king couldn't get over his joy and decided to give a great feast. He invited not only his relatives, friends, and acquaintances, but also the Wise Women, for he wanted them to feel friendly toward his child. There were thirteen Wise Women in his kingdom, but he only had twelve golden plates for them to eat from, so one of them had

---

1   First published in 1812/15, in the first edition of *Kinder- und Hausmärchen*. This text from the second edition (1819), from *Grimms' Tales for Young and Old*, trans. Ralph Manheim (Garden City, NY: Anchor P, 1977).

to stay home. The feast was celebrated in great splendour and when it was over the Wise Women gave the child their magic gifts; one gave virtue, the second beauty, the third wealth, and so on, until they had given everything a person could wish for in this world. When the eleventh had spoken, the thirteenth suddenly stepped in. She had come to avenge herself for not having been invited, and without a word of greeting, without so much as looking at anyone, she cried out in a loud voice: "When she is fifteen, the princess will prick her finger on a spinning wheel and fall down dead." Then without another word she turned around and left the hall. Everyone was horror-stricken. But the twelfth Wise Woman, who still had her wish to make, stepped forward, and since she couldn't undo the evil spell but only soften it, she said: "The princess will not die, but only fall into a deep hundred-year sleep."

The king, who wanted to guard his beloved child against such a calamity, sent out an order that every spindle in the whole kingdom should be destroyed. All the Wise Women's wishes for the child came true: she grew to be so beautiful, so modest, so sweet-tempered and wise that no one who saw her could help loving her. The day she turned fifteen the king and the queen happened to be away from home and she was left alone. She went all over the castle, examining room after room, and finally she came to an old tower. She climbed a narrow winding staircase, which led to a little door with a rusty key in the lock. She turned the key, the door sprang open, and there in a small room sat an old woman with a spindle, busily spinning her flax. "Good day, old woman," said the princess. "What are you doing?" "I'm spinning," said the old woman, nodding her head. "And what's the thing that twirls around so gaily?" the princess asked. With that she took hold of the spindle and tried to spin, but no sooner had she touched it than the magic spell took effect and she pricked her finger.

The moment she felt the prick she fell down on the bed that was in the room and a deep sleep came over her. And her sleep spread to the entire palace. The king and queen had just come home, and when they entered the great hall they fell asleep and the whole court with them. The horses fell asleep in the stables, the dogs in the courtyard, the pigeons on the roof, and the flies on the wall. Even the fire on the hearth stopped flaming and fell asleep, and the roast stopped crackling, and the cook, who was about to pull the kitchen boy's hair because he had done something wrong, let go and fell asleep. And the wind died down, and not a leaf stirred on the trees outside the castle.

All around the castle a brier hedge began to grow. Each year it grew higher until in the end it surrounded and covered the whole castle and there was no trace of a castle to be seen, not even the flag on the roof. The story of Brier Rose, as people called the beautiful sleeping princess, came to be told far and wide, and from time to time a prince tried to pass through the hedge into the castle. But none succeeded, for the brier bushes clung together as though they had hands, so the young men were caught and couldn't break loose and died a pitiful death. After many years another prince came to the country and heard an old man telling about the brier hedge that was said to conceal a castle, where a beautiful princess named Brier Rose had been sleeping for a hundred years, along with the king and the queen and their whole court. The old man had also heard from his grandfather that a number of princes had tried to pass through the brier hedge and had got caught in it and died a pitiful death. Then the young man said: "I'm not afraid. I will go and see the beautiful Brier Rose." The good man did his best to dissuade him, but the prince wouldn't listen.

It so happened that the hundred years had passed and the day had come for Brier Rose to wake up. As the king's son approached the brier hedge, the briers turned into big beautiful flowers, which opened of their own accord and let him through, then closed behind him to form a hedge again. In the courtyard he saw the horses and mottled hounds lying asleep, and on the roof pigeons were roosting with their heads under their wings. When he went into the castle, the flies were asleep on the wall, the cook in the kitchen was still holding out his hand as though to grab the kitchen boy, and the maid was sitting at the table with a black hen in front of her that needed plucking. Going farther, he saw the whole court asleep in the great hall, and on the dais beside the throne lay the king and the queen. On he went, and everything was so still that he could hear himself breathe. At last he came to the tower and opened the door to the little room where Brier Rose was sleeping. There she lay, so beautiful that he couldn't stop looking at her, and he bent down and kissed her. No sooner had his lips touched hers than Brier Rose opened her eyes, woke up, and smiled sweetly. They went downstairs together, and then the king and the queen and the whole court woke up, and they all looked at each other in amazement. The horses in the courtyard stood up and shook themselves; the hounds jumped to their feet and wagged their tails; the pigeons on the roof took their heads from under their wings, looked around and flew off into the fields; the flies on the wall started crawling, the fire in the kitchen flamed up and cooked the meal; the roast began to crackle again, the cook boxed the kitchen boy's ear so hard that he howled, and the maid plucked the chicken. The prince and Brier Rose were married in splendour, and they lived happily to the end of their lives.

THE NEAPOLITAN SOLDIER[1]

Italo Calvino

THREE SOLDIERS HAD DESERTED THEIR regiment and taken to the open road. One was a Roman, one a Florentine, while the smallest was a Neapolitan. After traveling far and wide, they were overtaken by darkness in a forest. The Roman, who was the oldest of the three, said, "Boys, this is no time for us all three to go to sleep. We must take turns keeping watch an hour at a time."

He volunteered for the first watch, and the other two threw down their knapsacks, unrolled their blankets, and went fast asleep. The watch was almost up, when out of the forest rushed a giant.

"What are you doing here?" he asked the soldier.

"None of your business," replied the soldier, without even bothering to turn around.

The giant lunged at him, but the soldier proved the swifter of the two by drawing his sword and cutting off the giant's head. Then he picked up the head with one hand and the body with the other and threw them into a nearby well. He carefully cleaned his sword, resheathed it, and called his companion who was supposed to keep the next watch. Before awakening him, though, he thought, I'd better say nothing about the giant, or this Florentine will take fright and flee. So when the Florentine was awake and asking, "Did you see anything?" the Roman replied, "Nothing at all, everything was as calm as could be." Then he went to sleep.

The Florentine began his watch, and when it was just about up, here came another giant exactly like the first, who asked, "What are you doing here?"

"That's no business of yours or anybody else's," answered the Florentine.

The giant sprang at him, but in a flash the soldier drew his sword and lopped off his head, which he picked up along with the body and threw into the well. His watch was up, and he thought, I'd better say nothing of this to the lily-livered Neapolitan. If he knew that things like this went on around here, he'd take to his heels and we'd never see him again.

So, when the Neapolitan asked, "Did you see any action?" the Florentine replied, "None at all, you've nothing to worry about." Then he went to sleep.

The Neapolitan watched for almost an hour, and the forest was perfectly still. Suddenly the leaves rustled and out ran a giant. "What are you doing here?"

"What business is it of yours?" replied the Neapolitan.

The giant held up a hand that would have squashed the Neapolitan flatter than a

---

1   From *Italian Folktales*, retold by Italo Calvino, trans. George Martin (New York: Pantheon, 1980).

pancake, had he not dodged it, brandished his sword, and swept off the giant's head, after which he threw the remains into the well.

It was the Roman's turn once more to keep watch, but the Neapolitan thought, I first want to see where the giant came from. He therefore plunged into the forest, spied a light, hastened toward it, and came to a cottage. Peeping through the key-hole, he saw three old women in conversation before the fireplace.

"It's already past midnight, and our husbands are not yet back," said one.

"Do you suppose something has happened to them?" asked another. "It might not be a bad idea," said the third, "to go after them. What do you say?"

"Let's go right now," said the first. "I'll carry the lantern that enables you to see a hundred miles ahead."

"And I'll bring the sword," said the second, "which in every sweep wipes out an army."

"And I'll bring the shotgun that can kill the she-wolf at the king's palace," said the third.

"Let's be on our way." At that, they threw open the door.

Hiding behind the doorpost with sword in hand, the Neapolitan was all ready for them. Out came the first woman holding the lantern, and swish! her head flew off before she could say a single "Amen." Out came the second, and swish! her soul sped to kingdom come. Out came the third and went the way of her sisters.

The soldier now had the witches' lantern, sword, and shotgun and decided to try them out immediately. "We'll just see if those three dotards were telling the truth." He raised the lantern and saw an army a hundred miles away besieging a castle, and chained on the balcony was a she-wolf with flaming eyes. "Let's just see how the sword works." He picked it up and swung it around, then raised the lantern once more and peered into space: every last warrior lay lifeless on the ground beside his splintered lance and dead horse. Then the Neapolitan picked up the gun and shot the she-wolf.

"Now I'll go and see everything from close up," he said.

He walked and walked and finally reached the castle. His knocks and calls all went unanswered. He went inside and walked through all the rooms, but saw no one until he came to the most beautiful chamber of all, where a lovely maiden sat sleep-ing in a plush armchair.

The soldier went up to her, but she continued to sleep. One of her slippers had dropped off her foot, and the soldier picked it up and put it in his pocket. Then he kissed her and tiptoed away.

He was no sooner gone than the sleeping maiden awakened. She called her maids of honor, who were also sleeping in the next room. They woke up and ran to the princess, exclaiming, "The spell is broken! The spell is broken! We have awakened! The princess has awakened! Who could the knight be who freed us?"

"Quick," said the princess, "look out the windows and see if you see anyone."

The maids looked out and saw the massacred army and the slain she-wolf. Then the princess said, "Hurry to His Majesty, my father, and tell him a brave knight came and defeated the army that held me prisoner, killed the she-wolf that stood guard over me, and broke the evil spell by kissing me." She glanced at her bare foot and added, "And then he went off with my left slipper."

Overjoyed, the king had notices posted all over town: WHOEVER COMES FORWARD AS MY DAUGHTER'S DELIVERER SHALL HAVE HER IN MARRIAGE, BE HE PRINCE OR PAUPER.

In the meantime the Neapolitan had gone back to his companions in broad daylight. When he awakened them, they asked immediately, "Why didn't you call us earlier? How many hours did you watch?"

But he wasn't about to tell them all that had happened and simply said, "I was so wide-awake I watched the rest of the night."

Time went by without bringing a soul to town to claim the princess as his rightful bride. "What can we do?" wondered the king.

The princess had an idea. "Papa, let's open a country inn and put up a sign that reads: HERE YOU CAN EAT, DRINK, AND SLEEP AT NO CHARGE for three days. That will draw many people, and we'll surely hear something important."

They opened the inn, with the king's daughter acting as innkeeper. Who should then come by but our three soldiers as hungry as bears, and singing as usual, in spite of hard times. They read the sign, and the Neapolitan said, "Boys, here you can eat and sleep for nothing."

"Don't believe a word of it," replied his companions. "They just say that, the better to cheat people."

But the princess-innkeeper came out and invited them in, assuring them of the truth of every word of the sign. They entered the inn, and the princess served them a supper fit for a king. Then she took a seat at their table and said, "Well, what news do you bring from the world outside? Way off in the country like this, I never know what's going on elsewhere."

"We have very little of interest to report, madam," answered the Roman who then smugly told of the time he was keeping watch when suddenly confronted by a giant whose head he cut off.

"Zounds!" exclaimed the Florentine. "I too had something similar happen to me," and he told about his giant.

"And you, sir?" said the princess to the Neapolitan. "Has nothing ever happened to you?"

His companions burst out laughing. "You don't think he would have anything to tell, do you? Our friend here is such a coward he'd run and hide for a whole week if he heard a leaf rustle in the dark."

"Don't belittle the poor boy like that," said the maiden, who insisted that he too tell something.

So the Neapolitan said, "If you really want the truth, I too was confronted by a giant while you two were sleeping and I killed him."

"Ha, ha, ha!" laughed his companions. "You'd die of fright if you so much as saw a giant! That's enough! We don't want to hear any more, we're going to bed." And they went off and left him with the princess.

She served him wine and coaxed him to go on with his story. Thus, little by little, he came out with everything—the three old women, the lantern, the shotgun, the sword, and the lovely maiden he had kissed as she slept, and her slipper he had carried off.

"Do you still have the slipper?"

"Here it is," replied the soldier drawing it from his pocket.

Overjoyed the princess kept filling his glass until he fell asleep, then said to her valet, "Take him to the bedchamber I prepared especially for him, remove his clothes, and put out kingly garb for him on the chair."

When the Neapolitan awakened next morning he was in a room decorated entirely in gold and brocade. He went to put on his clothes and found in their place robes for a king. He pinched himself to make sure he wasn't dreaming and, unable to make heads or tails of a thing, he rang the bell.

Four liveried servants entered and bowed down to him. "At Your Highness's service. Did Your Highness sleep well?"

The Neapolitan blinked. "Have you lost your mind? What highness are you talking about? Give me my things so I can get dressed, and be done with this comedy."

"Calm down, Highness. We are here to shave you and dress your hair."

"Where are my companions? Where did you put my things?"

"They are coming right away, you will have everything immediately, but allow us first to dress you, Highness."

Once he realized there was no getting around them, the soldier let the servants proceed: they shaved him, dressed his hair, and clothed him in a kingly outfit. Then they brought in his chocolate, cake, and sweets. After breakfast he said, "Am I going to see my companions or not?"

"Right away, Highness."

In came the Roman and the Florentine, whose mouths flew open when they saw him dressed in such finery. "What are you doing in that costume?"

"You tell me. Your guess is as good as mine."

"Goodness knows what you've cooked up!" replied his companions. "You must have told the lady some pretty tall tales last night!"

"For your information, I told no tall tales to anyone."

"So how do you account for what's happening now?"

"I'll explain," said the king, coming in just then with the princess in her finest robe. "My daughter was under a spell, and this young man set her free."

By questions and answers, they got the entire story.

"I am therefore making him my daughter's husband," said the king, "and my heir. As for yourselves, have no fears. You will become dukes, since had you not slain the other two giants, my daughter would not be free today."

The wedding was celebrated to the great joy of all, and followed by a grand feast.

On the menu was chicken à la king:
Long live the queen!
Long live the king!

THE NINTH CAPTAIN'S TALE[1]

Arabian Nights

THERE WAS ONCE A WOMAN who could not conceive, for all her husband's assaulting. So one day she prayed to Allah, saying, "Give me a daughter, even if she be not proof against the smell of flax!"

In speaking thus of the smell of flax she meant that she would have a daughter, even if the girl were so delicate and sensitive that the anodyne smell of flax would take hold of her throat and kill her.

Soon the woman conceived and easily bore a daughter, as fair as the rising moon, as pale and delicate as moonlight.

When little Sittukhan, for such they called her, grew to be ten years old, the sultan's son passed beneath her window and saw her and loved her, and went back ailing to the palace.

Doctor succeeded doctor fruitlessly beside his bed; but, at last, an old woman, who had been sent by the porter's wife, visited him and said, after close scrutiny, "You are in love, or else you have a friend who loves you."

---

1   From *The Book of the Thousand Nights and One Night*, trans. E. Powys Mather, 2nd ed. (London: Routledge and Kegan Paul, 1964).

"I am in love," he answered.

"Tell me her name," she begged, "for I may be a bond between you."

"She is the fair Sittukhan," he replied; and she comforted him, saying, "Refresh your eyes and tranquilize your heart, for I will bring you into her presence."

Then she departed and sought out the girl, who was taking the air before her mother's door. After compliment and greeting, she said, "Allah protect so much beauty, my daughter! Girls like you, and with such lovely fingers, should learn to spin flax; for there is no more delightful sight than a spindle in spindle fingers." Then she went away.

At once the girl went to her mother, saying, "Mother, take me to the mistress."

"What mistress?" asked her mother.

"The flax mistress," answered the girl.

"Do not say such a thing!" cried the woman. "Flax is a danger to you. Its smell is fatal to your breast, a touch of it will kill you."

But her daughter reassured her, saying, "I shall not die," and so wept and insisted, that her mother sent her to the flax mistress.

The white girl stayed there for a day, learning to spin; and her fellow pupils marveled at her beauty and the beauty of her fingers. But, when a morsel of flax entered behind one of her nails, she fell swooning to the floor.

They thought her dead and sent to her father and mother, saying, "Allah prolong your days! Come and take up your daughter, for she is dead."

The man and his wife tore their garments for the loss of their only joy, and went, beaten by the wind of calamity, to bury her. But the old woman met them, and said, "You are rich folk, and it would be shame on you to lay so fair a girl in dust."

"What shall we do then?" they asked, and she replied, "Build her a pavilion in the midst of the waves of the river and couch her there upon a bed, that you may come to visit her."

So they built a pavilion of marble, on columns rising out of the river, and planted a garden about it with green lawns, and set the girl upon an ivory bed, and came there many times to weep.

What happened next?

The old woman went to the king's son, who still lay sick of love, and said to him, "Come with me to see the maiden. She waits you, couched in a pavilion above the waves of the river."

The prince rose up and bade his father's wazir[1] come for a walk with him. The two went forth together and followed the old woman to the pavilion. Then the prince said, "Wait for me outside the door, for I shall not be long."

---

1   Wazir: Prime minister.

He entered the pavilion and began to weep by the ivory bed, recalling verses in the praise of so much beauty. He took the girl's hand to kiss it and, as he passed her slim white fingers through his own, noticed the morsel of flax lodged behind one of her nails. He wondered at this and delicately drew it forth.

At once the girl came out of her swoon and sat up upon the ivory bed. She smiled at the prince, and whispered, "Where am I?"

"You are with me," he answered, as he pressed her all against him. He kissed her and lay with her, and they stayed together for forty days and forty nights. Then the prince took leave of his love, saying, "My wazir is waiting outside the door. I will take him back to the palace and then return."

He found the wazir and walked with him across the garden towards the gate, until he was met by white roses growing with jasmine. The sight of these moved him, and he said to his companion, "The roses and the jasmine are white with the pallor of Sittukhan's cheeks! Wait here for three days longer, while I go to look upon the cheeks of Sittukhan."

He entered the pavilion again and stayed three days with Sittukhan, admiring the white roses and the jasmine of her cheeks.

Then he rejoined the wazir and walked with him across the garden towards the gate, until the carob, with its long black fruit, rose up to meet him. He was moved by the sight of it, and said, "The carobs are long and black like the brows of Sittukhan. O wazir, wait here for three more days, while I go to view Sittukhan's brows."

He entered the pavilion again and stayed three days with the girl, admiring her perfect brows, long and black like carobs hanging two by two.

Then he rejoined the wazir and walked with him towards the gate, until a springing fountain with its solitary jet rose up to meet him. He was moved by this sight and said to the wazir, "The jet of the fountain is as Sittukhan's waist. Wait here for three days longer, while I go to gaze again upon the waist of Sittukhan."

He went up into the pavilion and stayed three days with the girl, admiring her waist, for it was as the slim jet of the fountain.

Then he rejoined the wazir and walked with him across the garden towards the gate. But Sittukhan, when she saw her lover come again a third time, had said to herself, "What brings him back?" So now she followed him down the stairs of the pavilion, and hid behind the door which gave on the garden to see what she might see.

The prince happened to turn and catch sight of her face. He returned toward her, pale and distracted, and said sadly, "Sittukhan, Sittukhan, I shall never see you more, never, never again." Then he departed with the wazir, and his mind was made up that he would not return.

Sittukhan wandered in the garden, weeping, lonely and regretting that she was not dead in very truth. As she walked by the water, she saw something sparkle in the grass and, on raising it, found it to be a talismanic ring. She rubbed the engraved carnelian of it, and the ring spoke, saying, "Behold here am I! What do you wish?"

"O ring of Sulaiman," answered Sittukhan, "I require a palace next to the palace of the prince who used to love me, and a beauty greater than my own."

"Shut your eye and open it!" said the ring; and, when the girl had done so, she found herself in a magnificent palace, next to the palace of the prince. She looked in a mirror which was there and marveled at her beauty.

Then she leaned at the window until her false love should pass by on his horse. When the prince saw her, he did not know her; but he loved her and hastened to his mother, saying, "Have you not some very beautiful thing which you can take as a present to the lady who dwells in the new palace? And can you not beg her, at the same time, to marry me?"

"I have two pieces of royal brocade," answered his mother, "I will take them to her and urge your suit with them." Without losing an hour, the queen visited Sittukhan, and said to her, "My daughter, I pray you to accept this present, and to marry my son."

The girl called her negress and gave her the pieces of brocade, bidding her cut them up for floor cloths; so the queen became angry and returned to her own dwelling.

When the son learned that the woman of his love had destined the cloth of gold for menial service, he begged his mother to take some richer present, and the queen paid a second visit, carrying a necklace of unflawed emeralds.

"Accept this gift, my daughter, and marry my son," she said; and Sittukhan answered, "O lady, your present is accepted." Then she called her slave, saying, "Have the pigeons eaten yet?"

"Not yet, mistress," answered the slave.

"Take them these green trifles!" said Sittukhan.

When she heard this outrageous speech, the queen cried, "You have humbled us, my daughter. Now, at least, tell me plainly whether you wish to marry my son or no."

"If you desire me to marry him," answered Sittukhan, "bid him feign death, wrap him in seven winding-sheets, carry him in sad procession through the city, and let your people bury him in the garden of my palace."

"I will tell him your conditions," said the queen.

"What do you think!" cried the mother to her son, when she had returned to him. "If you wish to marry the girl, you must pretend to be dead, you must be wrapped in seven winding-sheets, you must be led in sad procession through the city, and you must be buried in her garden!"

"Is that all, dear mother?" asked the prince in great delight. "Then tear your clothes and weep, and cry, 'My son is dead!'"

The queen rent her garments and cried in a voice shrill with pain, "Calamity and woe! My son is dead!"

All the folk of the palace ran to that place and, seeing the prince stretched upon the floor with the queen weeping above him, washed the body and wrapped it in seven winding-sheets. Then the old men and the readers of the Koran came together and formed a procession, which went throughout the city, carrying the youth covered with precious shawls. Finally they set down their burden in Sittukhan's garden and went their way.

As soon as the last had departed, the girl, who had once died of a morsel of flax, whose cheeks were jasmine and white roses, whose brows were carobs two by two, whose waist was the slim jet of the fountain, went down to the prince and unwrapped the seven winding-sheets from about him, one by one.

Then "Is it you?" she said. "You are ready to go very far for women; you must be fond of them!" The prince bit his finger in confusion, but Sittukhan reassured him, saying, "It does not matter this time!"

And they dwelt together in love delight.

CINDERELLA

We turn next to versions of "Cinderella" which, with "Little Red Riding Hood" and "Sleeping Beauty," might be described as the core of the Western fairy-tale canon. As with the two previous tales, the abiding popularity of "Cinderella" raises the inevitable question: what is the explanation behind such success?

Part of the answer lies in the phrase that has entered the vernacular: "hers (or his!) is a real Cinderella story." It signifies that the individual has risen from obscurity and oppression to success and celebrity, perhaps with the implication that the good fortune is well-deserved. There can be little doubt that the attraction of this tale has a lot to do with its theme of virtue revealed and rewarded: it invites us to recall times when we felt ourselves unappreciated and rejected—and then to share Cinderella's satisfaction at being discovered as a true princess. (Hans Andersen taps into much the same feeling in "The Ugly Duckling.")

At this point, we should not be surprised to discover that Perrault's Cinderella is a rather passive young lady, no stranger to self-denial; she goes out of her way to assist her obnoxious stepsisters in preparing for the ball while denying that she has any right to such pleasures. On their departure, Cinderella collapses in tears, provoking the appearance of a fairy-tale *deus ex machina* in the shape of her fairy godmother, who provides her with all the accoutrements necessary for an impressive entry into high society.

It would be interesting to know what version Perrault used as the basis for "Cinderella," since in a number of respects it is quite unique. In no other tale, for example, do we find a fairy godmother transforming a pumpkin into a coach, mice into horses, or lizards into lackeys—and no other tale contains that famous glass slipper. The Russian tale "Vasilisa the Beautiful" stays much closer to its folk-tale origins, in that the heroine receives magical assistance from her dead mother in the form of a tiny doll that Vasilisa carries in her pocket. (This is a motif common to numerous versions of the tale; in the Grimms' version, for instance, the spirit of the dead mother takes the form of a hazel tree and a white bird.) Although Vasilisa is ultimately re-warded with a royal husband, she wins him in rather less glamorous fashion than does Cinderella—and only after surviving an encounter with the Baba Yaga, one of the most formidable "bad mothers" in all of fairy tale.

The world of "Cap o' Rushes" is somewhat reminiscent of that in "The Nea-politan Soldier" ("Sleeping Beauty" section), in that it shares the same earthy forthrightness—made the more obvious by the dialect that Joseph Jacobs (1854-1916) reproduced in his collection *English Fairy Tales* (1890). (One assumes that such was also the case in the original Italian of Calvino's tale; we must not forget the translator's involvement in many of these tales.) Here, too, there is a striking contrast between the bourgeois virtues of forbearance and self-denial displayed by Cinderella and the vigorous practicality of Cap o' Rushes as she deals with the challenges life throws in her path. Jacobs's tale contains some obvious differenc-es from Perrault's, the most immediately apparent being the absence of a wicked stepmother and stepsisters. The opening episode bears a striking resemblance, of course, to the scene in Shakespeare's *King Lear* in which the king's youngest daugh-ter, Cordelia, offers as honest and plain an answer to her father as Cap o' Rushes—with the same consequence. The point here, however, is that in Cap o' Rushes we have a no-nonsense heroine who reacts to her rejection by creating a plan and fol-lowing it through to a successful conclusion that not only brings her a husband but also reconciles her to her father. Although less well-known, "Cap o' Rushes" is a significant variant of the Cinderella story that can be found in many collections, including those of the Grimm Brothers ("All-Fur") and Charles Perrault ("Don-keyskin"), although it differs from the latter two in omitting the father's incestuous attraction to his daughter.

The resilience that we have noted in Cap o' Rushes can also be found in the hero-ines of the next two tales, "Little Gold Star" from New Mexico, and "The Little Red Fish and the Clog of Gold" from Iraq. Both girls accept the consequences of encour-aging their fathers to remarry ("I picked up the scorpion with my own hand, I'll save myself with my own mind."), and both receive unexpected assistance from Nature, in the shape of a bird and a fish—an intervention that proves to be a test of human compassion and humility that is central to fairy-tale morality. The ease with which the fairy tale moves between human and animal characters is surely an echo of the close dependence and interconnectedness that our rural ancestors assumed with the world around them.

The Iraqi tale demonstrates how important socio-cultural differences are in our understanding of variations between one version and another. Its editor points out that in Arab society the sexes are so strictly segregated before marriage that "... a token [in this case, the golden clog] can well be the inspiration to love, where seeing the girl herself is forbidden."[1] And she adds that it is natural for the prince to look to his mother for help in tracking down the elusive maiden, "… for a girl worth having would not be exposed to the sight of men outside her household and her family. In such circumstances the Cinderella story seems entirely realistic, and it is told in countless versions in the Arab world."[2]

Although some of the familiar elements in "The Indian Cinderella" may well be attributable to European influence, the fact remains that the flavor of this tale is quite different; it serves to remind us that the term "fairy tale" must have a broad definition if it is to include not only the stories from the Western tradition but also those from other continents and cultures. Unlike the familiar European versions, in which the prince must seek out his elusive bride, here the roles are reversed, although now the seeking becomes a test in itself. Deeply embedded in the natural world, this tale has an impressive mythic quality; the girl's discovery that Strong Wind draws his sled with the Rainbow and uses the Milky Way for his bowstring makes for an impressively large-scale climax to the story. Other unusual elements in this story are the symbolic bathing that transforms the young woman and the fact that, once married to Strong Wind, "she helped him to do great deeds."

The tales in this section illustrate the paradoxical truth that early publication does not necessarily indicate greater authenticity. When Perrault published his version of "Cinderella" over three hundred years ago, there was no general assumption that the original shape and context were worth preserving, whereas modern collectors and editors are diligent in retaining as much of the tale as is consistent with transforming the spoken into the written word (see Joe Hayes's extensive commentary on the background to "Little Gold Star"). Indeed, it is instructive to note the differences between these tales and that of Perrault, since the latter has unquestionably established itself as the most popular version of this classic tale.

---

1   Inea Bushnaq, *Arab Folktales* (New York; Pantheon, 1987) 155-56.
2   Ibid., 156.

CINDERELLA: OR THE LITTLE GLASS SLIPPER[1]

Charles Perrault

THERE ONCE LIVED A MAN who married twice, and his second wife was the haughtiest and most stuck-up woman in the world. She already had two daughters of her own and her children took after her in every way. Her new husband's first wife had given him a daughter of his own before she died, but she was a lovely and sweet-natured girl, very like her own natural mother, who had been a kind and gentle woman.

The second wedding was hardly over before the stepmother showed her true colours. Her new daughter was so lovable that she made her own children seem even more unpleasant by contrast; so she found the girl insufferable. She gave her all the rough work about the house to do, washing the pots and pans, cleaning out Madame's bedroom and those of her stepsisters, too. She slept at the top of the house, in a garret, on a thin, lumpy mattress, while her stepsisters had rooms with fitted carpets, soft beds and mirrors in which they could see themselves from head to foot. The poor girl bore everything patiently and dared not complain to her father because he would have lost his temper with her. His new wife ruled him with a rod of iron.

When the housework was all done, she would tuck herself away in the chimney corner to sit quietly among the cinders, the only place of privacy she could find, and so the family nicknamed her Cinderbritches. But the younger sister, who was less spiteful than the older one, changed her nickname to Cinderella. Yet even in her dirty clothes, Cinderella could not help but be a hundred times more beautiful than her sisters, however magnificently they dressed themselves up.

The king's son decided to hold a ball to which he invited all the aristocracy. Our two young ladies received their invitations, for they were well connected. Busy and happy, they set about choosing the dresses and hairstyles that would suit them best and that made more work for Cinderella, who had to iron her sisters' petticoats and starch their ruffles. They could talk about nothing except what they were going to wear.

"I shall wear my red velvet with the lace trimming," said the eldest. "Well, I shall wear just a simple skirt but put my coat with the golden flowers over it and, of course, there's always my diamond necklace, which is really rather special," said the youngest.

They sent for a good hairdresser to cut and curl their hair and they bought the best cosmetics. They called Cinderella to ask for her advice, because she had excellent taste. Cinderella helped them to look as pretty as they could and they were very glad of her assistance, although they did not show it.

---

1   First published in 1697. This text from *Sleeping Beauty and Other Favourite Fairy Tales*, trans. Angela Carter (London: Gollancz, 1982).

As she was combing their hair, they said to her:

"Cinderella, dear, wouldn't you like to go to the ball yourself?"

"Oh don't make fun of me, my ladies, how could I possibly go to the ball!"

"Quite right, too; everyone would laugh themselves silly to see Cinderbritches at a ball."

Any other girl but Cinderella would have made horrid tangles of their hair after that, out of spite; but she was kind, and resisted the temptation. The stepsisters could not eat for two days, they were so excited. They broke more than a dozen corset-laces because they pulled them in so tightly in order to make themselves look slender and they were always primping in front of the mirror.

At last the great day arrived. When they went off, Cinderella watched them until they were out of sight and then began to cry. Her godmother saw how she was crying and asked her what the matter was.

"I want…I want to…"

But Cinderella was crying so hard she could not get the words out. Her godmother was a fairy. She said: "I think you're crying because you want to go to the ball."

"Yes," said Cinderella, sighing.

"If you are a good girl, I'll send you there," said her godmother.

She took her into her own room and said:

"Go into the garden and pick me a pumpkin."

Cinderella went out to the garden and picked the finest pumpkin she could find. She took it to her godmother, although she could not imagine how a pumpkin was going to help her get to the ball. Her godmother hollowed out the pumpkin until there was nothing left but the shell, struck it with her ring—and instantly the pumpkin changed into a beautiful golden coach.

Then the godmother went to look in the mousetrap, and found six live mice there. She told Cinderella to lift up the lid of the trap enough to let the mice come out one by one and, as each mouse crept out, she struck it lightly with her ring. At the touch of the ring, each mouse changed into a carriage horse. Soon the coach had six dappled greys to draw it.

Then she asked herself what would do for a coachman.

"I'll go and see if there is a rat in the rat-trap," said Cinderella. "A rat would make a splendid coachman."

"Yes, indeed," said her godmother. "Go and see."

There were three fat rats in the rat-trap that Cinderella brought to her. One had particularly fine whiskers, so the godmother chose that one; when she struck him with her ring, he changed into a plump coachman who had the most imposing moustache you could wish to see.

"If you look behind the watering-can in the garden, you'll find six lizards," the godmother told Cinderella. "Bring them to me."

No sooner had Cinderella brought them to her godmother than the lizards were all changed into footmen, who stepped up behind the carriage in their laced uniforms and hung on as if they had done nothing else all their lives.

The fairy said to Cinderella:

"There you are! Now you can go to the ball. Aren't you pleased?"

"Yes, of course. But how can I possibly go to the ball in these wretched rags?"

The godmother had only to touch her with her ring and Cinderella's workaday overalls and apron changed into a dress of cloth of gold and silver, embroidered with precious stones. Then she gave her the prettiest pair of glass slippers. Now Cinderella was ready, she climbed into the coach; but her godmother told her she must be home by midnight because if she stayed at the ball one moment more, her coach would turn back into a pumpkin, her horses to mice, her footmen to lizards and her clothes back into overalls again.

She promised her godmother that she would be sure to return from the ball before midnight. Then she drove off. The king's son had been told that a great princess, hitherto unknown to anyone present, was about to arrive at the ball and ran to receive her. He himself helped her down from her carriage with his royal hand and led her into the ballroom where all the guests were assembled. As soon as they saw her, an enormous silence descended. The dancing ceased, the fiddlers forgot to ply their bows as the entire company gazed at this unknown lady. The only sound in the entire ballroom was a confused murmur:

"Oh, isn't she beautiful!"

Even the king himself, although he was an old man, could not help gazing at her and remarked to the queen that he had not seen such a lovely young lady for a long time. All the women studied her hair and her ball-gown attentively so that they would be able to copy them the next day, provided they could find such a capable hairdresser, such a skillful dressmaker, such magnificent silk.

The king's son seated her in the most honoured place and then led her on to the dance floor; she danced so gracefully, she was still more admired. Then there was a fine supper but the prince could not eat at all, he was too preoccupied with the young lady. She herself went and sat beside her sisters and devoted herself to entertaining them. She shared the oranges and lemons the prince had given her with them and that surprised them very much, for they did not recognise her.

While they were talking, Cinderella heard the chimes of the clock striking a quarter to twelve. She made a deep curtsey and then ran off as quickly as she could. As soon as she got home, she went to find her godmother and thanked her and told her how much she wanted to go to the ball that was to be given the following day, because the king's son had begged her to. While she was telling her godmother everything that had happened, her stepsisters knocked at the door. Cinderella hurried to let them in.

"What a long time you've been!" she said to them yawning, rubbing her eyes and stretching as if she could scarcely keep awake, although she had not wanted to sleep for a single moment since they had left the house.

"If you had come to the ball, you wouldn't have been sleepy!" said one of the sisters. "The most beautiful princess you ever saw arrived unexpectedly and she was so kind to us, she gave us oranges and lemons."

Cinderella asked the name of the princess but they told her nobody knew it, and the king's son was in great distress and would give anything to find out more about her. Cinderella smiled and said:

"Was she really so very beautiful? Goodness me, how lucky you are. And can I never see her for myself? What a shame! Miss Javotte, lend me that old yellow dress you wear around the house so that I can go to the ball tomorrow and see her for myself."

"What?" exclaimed Javotte. "Lend my dress to such a grubby little Cinderbritches as it is—it must think I've lost my reason!"

Cinderella had expected a refusal; and she would have been exceedingly embarrassed if her sister had relented and agreed to lend her a dress and taken her to the ball in it.

Next day, the sisters went off to the ball again. Cinderella went, too, but this time she was even more beautifully dressed than the first time. The king's son did not leave her side and never stopped paying her compliments so that the young girl was utterly absorbed in him and time passed so quickly that she thought it must still be only eleven o'clock when she heard the chimes of midnight. She sprang to her feet and darted off as lightly as a doe. The prince sprang after her but he could not catch her; in her flight, however, she let fall one of her glass slippers and the prince tenderly picked it up. Cinderella arrived home out of breath, without her carriage, without her footmen, in her dirty old clothes again; nothing remained of all her splendour but one of her little slippers, the pair of the one she had dropped. The prince asked the guards at the palace gate if they had seen a princess go out; they replied they had seen nobody leave the castle last night at midnight but a ragged young girl who looked more like a kitchen-maid than a fine lady.

When her sisters came home from the ball, Cinderella asked them if they had enjoyed themselves again; and had the beautiful princess been there? They said, yes; but she had fled at the very stroke of midnight, and so promptly that she had dropped one of her little glass slippers. The king's son had found it and never took his eyes off it for the rest of the evening, so plainly he was very much in love with the beautiful lady to whom it belonged.

They spoke the truth. A few days later, the king's son publicly announced that he would marry whoever possessed the foot for which the glass slipper had been made. They made a start by trying the slipper on the feet of all the princesses; then moved on to the duchesses, then to the rest of the court, but all in vain. At last they brought the slipper to the two sisters, who did all they could to squeeze their feet into the slipper but could not manage it, no matter how hard they tried. Cinderella watched them; she recognised her own slipper at once. She laughed, and said:

"I'd like to try and see if it might not fit me!"

Her sisters giggled and made fun of her but the gentleman who was in charge of the slipper trial looked at Cinderella carefully and saw how beautiful she was. Yes, he said; of course she could try on the slipper. He had received orders to try the slipper on the feet of every girl in the kingdom. He sat Cinderella down and, as soon as he saw her foot, he knew it would fit the slipper perfectly. The two sisters were very much astonished, but not half so astonished as they were when Cinderella took her own glass slipper from her pocket. At that the godmother appeared; she struck Cinderella's overalls with her ring and at once the old clothes were transformed to garments more magnificent than all her ball-dresses.

Then her sisters knew she had been the beautiful lady they had seen at the ball. They threw themselves at her feet to beg her to forgive them for all the bad treatment she had received from them. Cinderella raised them up and kissed them and said she forgave them with all her heart and wanted them only always to love her. Then, dressed in splendour, she was taken to the prince. He thought she was more beautiful than ever and married her a few days later. Cinderella, who was as good as she was beautiful, took her sisters to live in the palace and arranged for both of them to be married, on the same day, to great lords.

Moral

Beauty is a fine thing in a woman; it will always be admired. But charm is beyond price and worth more, in the long run. When her godmother dressed Cinderella up and told her how to behave at the ball, she instructed her in charm. Lovely ladies, this gift is worth more than a fancy hairdo; to win a heart, to reach a happy ending, charm is the true gift of the fairies. Without it, one can achieve nothing; with it, everything.

Another Moral
It is certainly a great advantage to be intelligent, brave, well-born, sensible and have other similar talents given only by heaven. But however great may be your god-given store, they will never help you to get on in the world unless you have either a godfather or a godmother to put them to work for you.

VASILISA THE BEAUTIFUL[1]

Aleksandr Afanas'ev

IN A CERTAIN KINGDOM THERE lived a merchant. Although he had been married for twelve years, he had only one daughter, called Vasilisa the Beautiful. When the girl was eight years old, her mother died. On her deathbed the merchant's wife called her daughter, took a doll from under her coverlet, gave it to the girl, and said: "Listen, Vasilisushka. Remember and heed my last words. I am dying, and together with my maternal blessing I leave you this doll. Always keep it with you and do not show it to anyone; if you get into trouble, give the doll food, and ask its advice. When it has eaten, it will tell you what to do in your trouble." Then the mother kissed her child and died.

After his wife's death the merchant mourned as is proper, and then began to think of marrying again. He was a handsome man and had no difficulty in finding a bride, but he liked best a certain widow. Because she was elderly and had two daughters of her own, of almost the same age as Vasilisa, he thought that she was an experienced housewife and mother. So he married her, but was deceived, for she did not turn out to be a good mother for his Vasilisa. Vasilisa was the most beautiful girl in the village; her stepmother and stepsisters were jealous of her beauty and tormented her by giving her all kinds of work to do, hoping that she would grow thin from toil and tanned from exposure to the wind and sun; in truth, she had a most miserable life. But Vasilisa bore all this without complaint and became lovelier and more buxom, every day, while the stepmother and her daughters grew thin and ugly from spite, although they always sat with folded hands, like ladies.

How did all this come about? Vasilisa was helped by her doll. Without its aid the girl could never have managed all that work. In return, Vasilisa sometimes did not

---

1   First published in 1855. This text from *Russian Fairy Tales*, trans. Norbert Guterman (New York: Pantheon, 1945).

eat, but kept the choicest morsels for her doll. And at night, when everyone was asleep, she would lock herself in the little room in which she lived, and would give the doll a treat, saying: "Now, little doll, eat, and listen to my troubles. I live in my father's house but am deprived of all joy; a wicked stepmother is driving me from the white world. Tell me how I should live and what I should do." The doll would eat, then would give her advice and comfort her in her trouble, and in the morning, she would perform all the chores for Vasilisa, who rested in the shade and picked flowers while the flower beds were weeded, the cabbage sprayed, the water brought in, and the stove fired. The doll even showed Vasilisa an herb that would protect her from sunburn. She led an easy life, thanks to her doll.

Several years went by. Vasilisa grew up and reached the marriage age. She was wooed by all the young men in the village, but no one would even look at the step-mother's daughters. The stepmother was more spiteful than ever, and her answer to all the suitors was: "I will not give the youngest in marriage before the elder ones." And each time she sent a suitor away, she vented her anger on Vasilisa in cruel blows.

One day the merchant had to leave home for a long time in order to trade in dis-tant lands. The stepmother moved to another house; near that house was a thick for-est, and in a glade of that forest stood a hut, and in the hut lived Baba Yaga. She never allowed anyone to come near her and ate human beings as if they were chickens. Having moved into the new house, the merchant's wife, hating Vasilisa, repeatedly sent the girl to the woods for one thing or another; but each time Vasilisa returned home safe and sound: her doll had shown her the way and kept her far from Baba Yaga's hut.

Autumn came. The stepmother gave evening work to all three maidens: the old-est had to make lace, the second to knit stockings, and Vasilisa had to spin; and each one had to finish her task. The stepmother put out the lights all over the house, leav-ing only one candle in the room where the girls worked, and went to bed. The girls worked. The candle began to smoke; one of the stepsisters took up a scissor to trim it, but instead, following her mother's order, she snuffed it out, as though inadver-tently. "What shall we do now?" said the girls. "There is no light in the house and our tasks are not finished. Someone must run to Baba Yaga and get some light." "The pins on my lace give me light," said the one who was making lace. "I shall not go." "I shall not go either," said the one who was knitting stockings, "my knitting needles give me light." "Then you must go," both of them cried to their stepsister. "Go to Baba Yaga!" And they pushed Vasilisa out of the room. She went into her own little room, put the supper she had prepared before her doll, and said: "Now dolly, eat, and aid me in my need. They are sending me to Baba Yaga for a light, and she will eat me up." The doll ate the supper and its eyes gleamed like two candles. "Fear not, Vasilisushka," it said. "Go where you are sent, only keep me with you all the time. With me in your pocket you will suffer no harm from Baba Yaga." Vasilisa made ready, put her doll in her pocket, and, having made the sign of the cross, went into the deep forest.

She walked in fear and trembling. Suddenly a horseman galloped past her: his face was white, he was dressed in white, his horse was white, and his horse's trappings were white—daybreak came to the woods.

She walked on farther, and a second horseman galloped past her: he was all red, he was dressed in red, and his horse was red—the sun began to rise.

Vasilisa walked the whole night and the whole day, and only on the following evening did she come to the glade where Baba Yaga's hut stood. The fence around the hut was made of human bones, and on the spikes were human skulls with staring eyes; the doors had human legs for doorposts, human hands for bolts, and a mouth with sharp teeth in place of a lock. Vasilisa was numb with horror and stood rooted to the spot. Suddenly another horseman rode by. He was all black, he was dressed in black, and his horse was black. He galloped up to Baba Yaga's door and vanished, as though the earth had swallowed him up—night came. But the darkness did not last long. The eyes of all the skulls on the fence began to gleam and the glade was as bright as day. Vasilisa shuddered with fear, but not knowing where to run, remained on the spot.

Soon a terrible noise resounded through the woods; the trees crackled, the dry leaves rustled; from the woods Baba Yaga drove out in a mortar, prodding it on with a pestle, and sweeping her traces with a broom. She rode up to the gate, stopped, and sniffing the air around her, cried: "Fie, fie! I smell a Russian smell! Who is here?" Vasilisa came up to the old witch and, trembling with fear, bowed low to her and said: "It is I, grandmother. My stepsisters sent me to get some light." "Very well," said Baba Yaga. "I know them, but before I give you the light you must live with me and work for me; if not, I will eat you up." Then she turned to the gate and cried: "Hey, my strong bolts, unlock! Open up, my wide gate!" The gate opened, and Baba Yaga drove in whistling. Vasilisa followed her, and then everything closed again.

Having entered the room, Baba Yaga stretched herself out in her chair and said to Vasilisa: "Serve me what is in the stove; I am hungry." Vasilisa lit a torch from the skulls on the fence and began to serve Yaga the food from the stove—and enough food had been prepared for ten people. She brought kvass, mead, beer, and wine from the cellar. The old witch ate and drank everything, leaving for Vasilisa only a little cabbage soup, a crust of bread, and a piece of pork. Then Baba Yaga made ready to go to bed and said: "Tomorrow after I go, see to it that you sweep the yard, clean the hut, cook the dinner, wash the linen, and go to the cornbin and sort out a bushel of wheat. And let everything be done, or I will eat you up!" Having given these orders, Baba Yaga began to snore. Vasilisa set the remnants of the old witch's supper before her doll, wept bitter tears, and said: "Here dolly, eat, and aid me in my need!

Baba Yaga has given me a hard task to do and threatens to eat me up if I do not do it all. Help me!" The doll answered: "Fear not, Vasilisa the Beautiful! Eat your supper, say your prayers, and go to sleep; the morning is wiser than the evening."

Very early next morning Vasilisa awoke, after Baba Yaga had arisen, and looked out of the window. The eyes of the skulls were going out; then the white horseman flashed by, and it was daybreak. Baba Yaga went out into the yard, whistled, and the mortar, pestle, and broom appeared before her. The red horseman flashed by, and the sun rose. Baba Yaga sat in the mortar, prodded it on with the pestle, and swept her traces with the broom. Vasilisa remained alone, looked about Baba Yaga's hut, was amazed at the abundance of everything, and stopped wondering which work she should do first. For lo and behold, all the work was done; the doll was picking the last shreds of chaff from the wheat. "Ah my savior," said Vasilisa to her doll, "you have delivered me from death." "All you have to do," answered the doll, creeping into Vasilisa's pocket, "is to cook the dinner; cook it with the help of God and then rest, for your health's sake."

When evening came Vasilisa set the table and waited for Baba Yaga. Dusk began to fall, the black horseman flashed by the gate, and night came; only the skulls' eyes were shining. The trees crackled, the leaves rustled; Baba Yaga was coming. Vasilisa met her. "Is everything done?" asked Yaga. "Please see for yourself, grandmother," said Vasilisa. Baba Yaga looked at everything, was annoyed that there was nothing she could complain about, and said: "Very well, then." Then she cried: "My faithful servants, my dear friends, grind my wheat!" Three pairs of hands appeared, took the wheat, and carried it out of sight. Baba Yaga ate her fill, made ready to go to sleep, and again gave her orders to Vasilisa. "Tomorrow," she commanded, "do the same work you have done today, and in addition take the poppy seed from the bin and get rid of the dust, grain by grain; someone threw dust into the bins out of spite." Having said this, the old witch turned to the wall and began to snore, and Vasilisa set about feeding her doll. The doll ate, and spoke as she had spoken the day before: "Pray to God and go to sleep; the morning is wiser than the evening. Everything will be done, Vasilisushka."

Next morning Baba Yaga again left the yard in her mortar, and Vasilisa and the doll soon had all the work done. The old witch came back, looked at everything, and cried: "My faithful servants, my dear friends, press the oil out of the poppy seed!" Three pairs of hands appeared, took the poppy seed, and carried it out of sight. Baba Yaga sat down to dine; she ate, and Vasilisa stood silent. "Why do you not speak to me?" said Baba Yaga. "You stand there as though you were dumb." "I did not dare to speak," said Vasilisa, "but if you'll give me leave, I'd like to ask you something." "Go ahead. But not every question has a good answer; if you know too much, you will soon grow old." "I want to ask you, grandmother, only about what I have seen. As I was on my way to you, a horseman on a white horse, all white himself and dressed in white, overtook me. Who is he?" "He is my bright day," said Baba Yaga. "Then another horseman overtook me; he had a red horse, was red himself, and was dressed in red. Who is he?" "He is my red sun." "And who is the black horseman whom I met at your very gate, grandmother?" "He is my dark night—and all of them are my faithful servants."

Vasilisa remembered the three pairs of hands, but kept silent. "Why don't you ask me more?" said Baba Yaga. "That will be enough," Vasilisa replied. "You said yourself, grandmother, that one who knows too much will grow old soon." "It is well," said Baba Yaga, "that you ask only about what you have seen outside my house, not inside my house; I do not like to have my dirty linen washed in public, and I eat the over-curious. Now I shall ask you something. How do you manage to do the work I set for you?" "I am helped by the blessing of my mother," said Vasilisa. "So that is what it is," shrieked Baba Yaga. "Get you gone, blessed daughter! I want no blessed ones in my house!" She dragged Vasilisa out of the room and pushed her outside the gate, took a skull with burning eyes from the fence, stuck it on a stick, and gave it to the girl, saying: "Here is your light for your stepsisters. Take it; that is what they sent you for."

Vasilisa ran homeward by the light of the skull, which went out only at daybreak, and by nightfall of the following day she reached the house. As she approached the gate, she was about to throw the skull away, thinking that surely they no longer needed a light in the house. But suddenly a dull voice came from the skull, saying "Do not throw me away, take me to your stepmother." She looked at the stepmother's house and, seeing that there was no light in the windows, decided to enter with her skull. For the first time she was received kindly. Her stepmother and stepsisters told her that since she had left they had had no fire in the house; they were unable to strike a flame themselves, and whatever light was brought by the neighbors went out the moment it was brought into the house. "Perhaps your fire will last," said the stepmother. The skull was brought into the room, and its eyes kept staring at the stepmother and her daughters, and burned them. They tried to hide, but wherever they went the eyes followed them. By morning they were all burned to ashes; only Vasilisa remained untouched by the fire.

In the morning Vasilisa buried the skull in the ground, locked up the house, and went to the town. A certain childless old woman gave her shelter, and there she lived, waiting for her father's return. One day she said to the woman: "I am weary of sitting without work, grandmother. Buy me some flax, the best you can get; at least I shall be spinning." The old woman bought good flax and Vasilisa set to work. She spun as fast as lightning and her threads were even and thin as a hair. She spun a great deal of yarn; it was time to start weaving it, but no comb fine enough for Vasilisa's yarn could be found, and no one would undertake to make one. Vasilisa asked her doll for aid. The doll said: "Bring me an old comb, an old shuttle, and a horse's mane; I will make a loom for you." Vasilisa got everything that was required and went to sleep, and during the night the doll made a wonderful loom for her.

By the end of the winter the linen was woven, and it was so fine that it could be passed through a needle like a thread. In the spring the linen was bleached, and Vasilisa said to the old woman: "Grandmother, sell this linen and keep the money for yourself." The old woman looked at the linen and gasped: "No, my child! No one can wear such linen except the tsar; I shall take it to the palace." The old woman went to the tsar's palace and walked back and forth beneath the windows. The tsar saw her and asked: "What do you want, old woman?" "Your Majesty," she answered, "I have brought rare merchandise; I do not want to show it to anyone but you." The tsar ordered her to be brought before him, and when he saw the linen he was amazed. "What do you want for it?" asked the tsar. "It has no price, little father tsar! I have brought it as a gift to you." The tsar thanked her and rewarded her with gifts.

The tsar ordered shirts to be made of the linen. It was cut, but nowhere could they find a seamstress who was willing to sew them. For a long time they tried to find one, but in the end the tsar summoned the old woman and said: "You have known how to spin and weave such linen, you must know how to sew shirts of it." "It was not I that spun and wove this linen, Your Majesty," said the old woman. "This is the work of a maiden to whom I give shelter." "Then let her sew the shirts," ordered the tsar.

The old woman returned home and told everything to Vasilisa. "I knew all the time," said Vasilisa to her, "that I would have to do this work." She locked herself in her room and set to work; she sewed without rest and soon a dozen shirts were ready. The old woman took them to the tsar, and Vasilisa washed herself, combed her hair, dressed in her finest clothes, and sat at the window. She sat there waiting to see what would happen. She saw a servant of the tsar entering the courtyard. The messenger came into the room and said: "The tsar wishes to see the needlewoman who made his shirts, and wishes to reward her with his own hands." Vasilisa appeared before the tsar. When the tsar saw Vasilisa the Beautiful he fell madly in love with her. "No, my beauty," he said, "I will not separate from you; you shall be my wife." He took Vasilisa by her white hands, seated her by his side, and the wedding was celebrated at once. Soon Vasilisa's father returned, was overjoyed at her good fortune, and came to live in his daughter's house. Vasilisa took the old woman into her home too, and carried her doll in her pocket till the end of her life.

CAP O' RUSHES[1]

Joseph Jacobs

WELL, THERE WAS ONCE A very rich gentleman, and he'd three daughters, and he thought he'd see how fond they were of him. So he says to the first, "How much do you love me, my dear?" "Why," says she, "as I love my life." "That's good," says he.

So he says to the second, "How much do *you* love me, my dear?"

"Why," says she, "better nor all the world."

"That's good," says he. So he says to the third, "How much do *you* love me, my dear?"

"Why, I love you as fresh meat loves salt," says she.

Well, but he was angry. "You don't love me at all," says he, "and in my house you stay no more." So he drove her out there and then, and shut the door in her face.

Well, she went away on and on till she came to a fen,[2] and there she gathered a lot of rushes and made them into a kind of a sort of a cloak with a hood, to cover her from head to foot, and to hide her fine clothes. And then she went on and on till she came to a great house.

"Do you want a maid?" says she.

"No, we don't," said they.

"I haven't nowhere to go," says she; "and I ask no wages, and do any sort of work," says she.

"Well," said they, "if you like to wash the pots and scrape the saucepans you may stay," said they.

So she stayed there and washed the pots and scraped the saucepans and did all the dirty work. And because she gave no name they called her "Cap o' Rushes."

Well, one day there was to be a great dance a little way off, and the servants were allowed to go and look on at the grand people. Cap o' Rushes said she was too tired to go, so she stayed at home.

But when they were gone she offed with her cap o' rushes, and cleaned herself, and went to the dance. And no one there was so finely dressed as she.

Well, who should be there but her master's son, and what should he do but fall in love with her the minute he set eyes on her. He wouldn't dance with any one else.

But before the dance was done Cap o' Rushes slipped off, and away she went home. And when the other maids came back she was pretending to be asleep with her cap o' rushes on.

Well, next morning they said to her, "You did miss a sight, Cap o' Rushes!"

1 From *English Fairy Tales*, 1890 (repr. New York: Dover, 1967).
2 Fen: Bog or marsh.

"What was that?" says she.

"Why, the beautifullest lady you ever see, dressed right gay and ga'.[1] The young master, he never took his eyes off her." "Well, I should have liked to have seen her," says Cap o' Rushes. "Well, there's to be another dance this evening, and perhaps she'll be there."

But, come the evening, Cap o' Rushes said she was too tired to go with them. Howsoever, when they were gone she offed with her cap o' rushes and cleaned herself, and away she went to the dance.

The master's son had been reckoning on seeing her, and he danced with no one else, and never took his eyes off her. But, before the dance was over, she slipped off, and home she went, and when the maids came back she pretended to be asleep with her cap o' rushes on.

Next day they said to her again, "Well, Cap o' Rushes, you should ha' been there to see the lady. There she was again, gay and ga', and the young master he never took his eyes off her."

"Well, there," says she, "I should ha' liked to ha' seen her."

"Well," says they, "there's a dance again this evening, and you must go with us, for she's sure to be there."

Well, come this evening, Cap o' Rushes said she was too tired to go, and do what they would she stayed at home. But when they were gone she offed with her cap o' rushes and cleaned herself, and away she went to the dance.

The master's son was rarely glad when he saw her. He danced with none but her and never took his eyes off her. When she wouldn't tell him her name, nor where she came from, he gave her a ring and told her if he didn't see her again he should die.

Well, before the dance was over, off she slipped, and home she went, and when the maids came home she was pretending to be asleep with her cap o' rushes on.

Well, next day they says to her, "There, Cap o' Rushes, you didn't come last night, and now you won't see the lady, for there's no more dances."

"Well I should have rarely liked to have seen her," says she.

The master's son he tried every way to find out where the lady was gone, but go where he might, and ask whom he might, he never heard anything about her. And he got worse and worse for the love of her till he had to keep his bed.

"Make some gruel for the young master," they said to the cook. "He's dying for the love of the lady." The cook she set about making it when Cap o' Rushes came in.

"What are you adoing of?" says she.

"I'm going to make some gruel for the young master," says the cook, "for he's dying for love of the lady."

---

1   And ga': And all (colloquial).

"Let me make it," says Cap o' Rushes.

Well, the cook wouldn't at first, but at last she said yes, and Cap o' Rushes made the gruel. And when she had made it she slipped the ring into it on the sly before the cook took it upstairs.

The young man he drank it and then he saw the ring at the bottom.

"Send for the cook," says he.

So up she comes.

"Who made this gruel here?" says he.

"I did," says the cook, for she was frightened.

And he looked at her.

"No, you didn't," says he. "Say who did it, and you shan't be harmed."

"Well, then, 'twas Cap o' Rushes," says she.

"Send Cap o' Rushes here," says he. So Cap o' Rushes came.

"Did you make my gruel?" says he.

"Yes, I did," says she.

"Where did you get this ring?" says he.

"From him that gave it me," says she.

"Who are you, then?" says the young man.

"I'll show you," says she. And she offed with her cap o' rushes, and there she was in her beautiful clothes.

Well, the master's son he got well very soon, and they were to be married in a little time. It was to be a very grand wedding, and every one was asked far and near. And Cap o' Rushes' father was asked. But she never told anybody who she was.

But before the wedding she went to the cook, and says she:

"I want you to dress every dish without a mite o' salt."

"That'll be rare nasty," says the cook.

"That doesn't signify," says she.

"Very well," says the cook.

Well, the wedding-day came, and they were married. And after they were married all the company sat down to the dinner. When they began to eat the meat, it was so tasteless they couldn't eat it. But Cap o' Rushes' father tried first one dish and then another, and then he burst out crying.

"What is the matter?" said the master's son to him.

"Oh!" says he, "I had a daughter. And I asked her how much she loved me. And she said 'As much as fresh meat loves salt.' And I turned her from my door, for I thought she didn't love me. And now I see she loved me best of all. And she may be dead for aught I know."

"No, father, here she is!" says Cap o' Rushes. And she goes up to him and puts her arms round him. And so they were all happy ever after.

LITTLE GOLD STAR[1]

Joe Hayes

LONG, LONG AGO THERE LIVED a man whose wife had died. The only family he had was a daughter whose name was Arcia. The man's neighbor was a woman named Margarita, and her husband had died. Margarita had two daughters.

Every day when Arcia would walk down the street in front of Margarita's house, the neighbor would come out and give her something good to eat. She'd give her pan *dulce* or cookies or little honey cakes.

One day Arcia said to her father, "Papa, why don't you marry our neighbor. She's very good to me. She gives me something sweet to eat almost very day."

Her father didn't want to do it. "You'll see, daughter, he said to Arcia—

Today Margarita is so sweet and kind,
But her sweetness will turn bitter with time."

But Arcia insisted. "No! She's a nice woman, and you should marry her." Finally she got her way, and her father married their neighbor.

At first everything was fine. But when summer came and the man went off to the mountains to take his sheep to the high meadows, the stepsisters started quarreling with Arcia.

Margarita no longer liked Arcia. She was very unkind to her. She bought many beautiful gifts for her own daughters—silken dresses and gold jewelry—but when Arcia's shoes wore out, she didn't even buy her a new pair. Arcia had to go around barefoot.

In time the bedroom was so full of the beautiful things of the stepsisters that there was no room for Arcia to sleep there. She had to move to the kitchen and sleep next to the stove.

When Arcia's father returned from the mountains, he chose three young sheep from the flock. He gave one sheep to each girl. "Tend your sheep carefully," he told them. "When they're full grown, you can sell them and keep the money yourselves. Or, if you wish, I'll shear the sheep and you can spin and weave the wool."

The girls began tending their sheep, and Arcia took the best care of hers. Before long it was the fattest of the three and covered with thick wool.

One day Arcia said to her father, "Papa, I want you to shear my sheep for me.

---

1   Published in 2000 (El Paso, Cinco Puntos P).

I'll spin the wool and weave it into a blanket to keep you warm when you go to the mountains."

So the man sheared his daughter's sheep and Arcia carried the wool down to the river to wash it. She was bending over, washing the wool in the water of the stream, when suddenly a big hawk came swooping down from the sky and snatched it away from her.

Arcia called out to the bird, "Señor Hawk, please give my wool back to me."

And the hawk replied to her with human speech: "Lift ... up ... your ... eyes ... Look ... where ... I ... fly-y-y."

So she did what the bird had told her to do. She turned her head and looked up. When she looked up, down from the sky came a little gold star, and it fastened itself to her forehead.

She went running home, and as she ran along, the wool fell into her arms, already washed and spun and woven into fine cloth.

When she got home Margarita said, "Take that piece of tin off your forehead!" And she grabbed her and tried to scrape the star off, but the more she scraped, the more brightly it shone.

Her stepsisters were filled with jealousy. They said, "Why shouldn't we have a star on our foreheads too?" And they went looking for their stepfather to have him shear their sheep.

The first one found him and ordered him to shear her sheep. She went running to the river with the wool. As she was washing it in the water of the stream, the hawk came swooping down again and snatched it away.

"You evil bird!" she screamed. "Bring my wool back to me."

The hawk called down, "Lift ... up ... your ... eyes ... Look ... where ... I ... fly-y-y."

"What?" she said. "Don't tell me where to look. I'll look wherever I want to. Bring my wool back right now."

But finally she had to look up to see where the hawk had gone. When she did look up, down from the sky came a long floppy donkey's ear and fastened itself to her forehead!

The girl ran home crying. When her mother saw her she gasped, "Bring me my scissors!" She took her scissors and snipped off the donkey's ear, but a longer and floppier one grew in its place.

From that day on, everyone in the village called the girl *Donkey Ear*!

But the other sister didn't know what had happened, and she went to the river with the wool from her sheep. She started to wash it in the water, and again the hawk swooped down and snatched it away.

"You rotten hawk," she shouted. "Bring my wool back."

"Lift … up … your … eyes…. Look … where … I … fly-y-y."

"I don't have to obey you. Bring my wool back this instant!"

But she too had to look up to find out where the hawk had gone. When she looked up, down from the sky came a long, green cow horn, and it stuck to her forehead.

She ran home, and when her mother saw her, she said, "Bring me a saw!"

With the saw she tried to cut the cow horn off, but the more she cut, the longer and greener it grew. From that day on, everyone in the village called her *Green Horn*!

But all the villagers called Arcia *Little Gold Star*. And so Margarita wouldn't let Arcia go to town anymore. She made her stay home and do all the work. She had to cook supper and clean the house and wash the clothes. She had to chop firewood and carry water from the well.

And then one day when Arcia was going to the well with her bucket, a messenger from the king's palace came by. He was spreading the word that the prince had decided he would like to get married. Since he couldn't find any girl in his own village to fall in love with, he thought he'd give a big party. Every girl from every village throughout the mountains was invited so that the prince could find a bride.

Arcia told her stepsisters what she had heard, and when the day of the party arrived, she helped them get dressed in their silken gowns. She fixed their hair for them so that it would hide the horrible things on their foreheads. She went to the door and waved goodbye as they went off to the party. She didn't even have a pair of shoes, much less a fancy dress for a party, so she had to stay home.

But that evening, all by herself at home, she began to feel sad. She thought, *It won't do any harm if I just go to the palace and look in the window to see what a fine party is like.*

She went to the palace and crept up to the window and peeked in. When she peeked through the window, the little gold star on her forehead began to shine more brightly than the sun. Everyone turned to look.

The prince called out, "Have the girl with the gold star come in here!" And his servants went running to bring Arcia into the party. But when Arcia saw the servants, she was frightened and ran home.

The next day, the prince and his servants started going from house to house looking for the girl with the gold star. Finally they came to Arcia's house. But Margarita made her hide under the table in the kitchen and ordered her not to come out.

The woman called for her own daughters and presented them to the prince. "Your Majesty, one of these might be the girl you're looking for. Aren't they lovely young women?"

The prince took one look at the girls and gasped. He saw the cow horn and the donkey ear on their foreheads.

"No, señora," the prince said politely. "I don't think either one is the girl I'm looking for." And he started backing toward the door.

But just then the cat got up from her bed by the fireplace and walked toward the prince. The cat rubbed against the prince's ankle and purred, "Meeooow … meeooow … Arcia is hiding under the table."

"What was that?" the prince asked. "Did the cat say someone is under the table?"

"Oh, no," the woman said. "The cat's just hungry." She picked up the cat and threw it outside.

But the cat came right back and rubbed against the prince's other ankle. "Meeooow … meeooow … Arcia is hiding under the table."

"Yes!" the prince insisted. "The cat said someone is under the table. Who is it?" And he told his servants to find out.

When Arcia saw the servants coming toward her, she stood up. Even in her dirty, ragged old clothes she looked as fine and noble as a princess. The prince fell in love with her at first sight.

The prince asked Arcia to marry him, and she said she would. A few days later, the wedding celebration began. It lasted for nine days and nine nights, and the last day was better than the first. And everyone was invited, even the mean Margarita and her two daughters—*Green Horn* and *Donkey Ear*!

I came on a colt
And I'll leave on its mother.
If you liked this story
Then tell me another!

Note for Readers and Storytellers

This Cinderella *cuento* was extremely popular in the mountain communities of New Mexico. All the traditional versions influenced my treatment of the tale, but I especially relied on that of Aurora Lucero White Lea in *Literary Folklore of the Hispanic Southwest*. It is from her version that I got the name Arcia. The traditional versions are consistent in many details and I've tried to retain what I see as essential to the story. The symbolic reward of a gold star on the forehead appears in almost every version of the Cinderella tale in New Mexico. It appears in other tales as well, but it seems especially central to this tale.

One way in which many traditional tellings differ from mine is that the animal which snatches the object away from the girls is most often a fish, rather than a bird. And in most versions the sheep is slaughtered and the sheep's intestines stolen, but I thought this detail was a bit gruesome [for a fully illustrated picture book]. Another element found in many traditional Hispanic tellings, but not in mine, is the appearance of the Blessed Virgin to advise the girls. Of course, only the heroine heeds her advice. I assume she is the same figure who is identified as the Fairy God-mother in the best-known version of Cinderella. I base my telling on a plot form that doesn't require her intervention.

As in my story, almost all traditional versions of the tale give the father's response to the daughter's request that he marry their neighbor in verse form, most commonly

Si hoy nos da sopitas de miel
(Though she gives us bread pudding with honey today,)
Manana nos dara sopitas de hiel.
(Tomorrow she'll give us bread pudding with gall.)

This is a folk expression once fairly popular in New Mexico. The figurative mean-ing of *sopitas de miel* is roughly equivalent to the contemporary English expression, *nicey-nice*. And of course *sopitas de hiel* means the opposite. I changed the verse to one I learned from a teacher at the elementary school in Taos, New Mexico. The po-etic elements of the Spanish make it more fun to say. But even more important to me is the name it provides for the stepmother. By referring to her as Margarita, rather than the stepmother, I was able to avoid something that causes some contemporary readers and listeners discomfort: the association of so many negative descriptors with the word stepmother in the old tales.

The little verse on the end of the story is more than decoration. Because the old cuentos date from a time when storytelling was a very important activity, they bear remnants of the rituals and form as that accompanied the telling of tales. It was once customary to end each story with a brief verse, just as many people still end every prayer with the word *amen.*

THE LITTLE RED FISH AND THE CLOG OF GOLD[1]
Inea Bushnaq

NEITHER HERE NOR THERE LIVED a man, a fisherman. His wife had drowned in the great river and left him a pretty little girl not more than two years old. In a house nearby lived a widow and her daughter. The women began to come to the fisherman's house to care for the girl and comb her hair, and every time she said to

---

1   From *Arab Folktales* (New York: Pantheon Books, 1986).

the child, "Am I not like a mother to you?" She tried to please the fisherman, but he always said, "I shall never marry. Stepmothers hate their husband's children even though their rivals are dead and buried." When his daughter grew old enough to pity him when she saw him washing his own clothes, she began to say, "Why don't you marry our neighbor, Father? There is no evil in her, and she loves me as much as her own daughter."

They say water will wear away stone. In the end the fisherman married the widow, and she came to live in his house. The wedding week was not yet over when sure enough, she began to feel jealous of her husband's daughter. She saw how much her father loved the child and indulged her. And she could not help but see that the child was fair, and quick, while her own daughter was thin and sallow, and so clumsy she did not know how to sew the seam of her gown.

No sooner did the woman feel that she was mistress of the house than she began to leave all the work for the girl to do. She would not give her stepchild soap to wash her hair and feet, and she fed her nothing but crusts and crumbs. All this the girl bore patiently, saying not a word. For she did not wish to grieve her father, and she thought, "I picked up the scorpion with my own hand; I'll save myself with my own mind."

Besides her other errands, the fisherman's daughter had to go down to the river each day to bring home her father's catch, the fish they ate and sold. One day from beneath a basket load of three catfish, suddenly one little red fish spoke to her:

Child with such patience to endure,
I beg you now, my life secure.
Throw me back into the water,
And now and always be my daughter.

The girl stopped to listen, half in wonder and half in fear. Then retracing her steps, she flung the fish into the river and said, "Go! People say, 'Do a good deed for, even if it is like throwing gold into the sea, in God's sight it is not lost.'" And lifting itself on the face of the water, the little fish replied:

Your kindness is not in vain—
A new mother do you gain.
Come to me when you are sad,
And I shall help to make you glad.

The girl went back to the house and gave the three catfish to her stepmother. When the fisherman returned and asked about the fourth, she told him, "Father, the red fish dropped from my basket. It may have fallen into the river, for I couldn't find it again." "Never mind," he said, "it was a very small fish." But her stepmother began to scold. "You never told me there were four fishes. You never said that you lost one. Go now and look for it, before I curse you!"

It was past sunset and the girl had to walk back to the river in the dark. Her eyes swollen with tears, she stood on the water's edge and called out,

Red fish, my mother and nurse,
Come quickly, and ward off a curse.

And there at her feet appeared the little red fish to comfort her and say, "Though patience is bitter, its fruit is very sweet. Now bend down and take this gold piece from my mouth. Give it to your stepmother, and she will say nothing to you." Which is exactly what happened.

The years came and the years went, and in the fisherman's house life continued as before. Nothing changed except that the two little girls were now young women.

One day a great man, the master of the merchants' guild, announced that his daughter was to be married. It was the custom for the women to gather at the bride's house on the "day of the bride's henna" to celebrate and sing as they watched the girl's feet, palms, and arms being decorated for the wedding with red henna stain. Then every mother brought her unwed daughters to be seen by the mothers of sons. Many a girl's destiny was decided on such a day.

The fisherman's wife rubbed and scrubbed her daughter and dressed her in her finest gown and hurried her off to the master merchant's house with the rest. The fisherman's daughter was left at home to fill the water jar and sweep the floor while they were gone.

But as soon as the two women were out of sight, the fisherman's daughter gathered up her gown and ran down to the river to tell the little red fish her sorrow. "You shall go to the bride's henna and sit on the cushions in the center of the hall," said the little red fish. She gave the girl a small bundle and said, "Here is everything you need to wear, with a comb of pearl for your hair and clogs of gold for your feet. But one thing you must remember: be sure to leave before your stepmother rises to go."

When the girl loosened the cloth that was knotted round the clothes, out fell a gown of silk as green as clover. It was stitched with threads and sequins of gold, and from its folds rose a sweet smell like the essence of roses. Quickly she washed herself and decked herself and tucked the comb of pearl behind her braid and slipped the golden clogs onto her feet and went tripping off to the feast.

The women from every house in the town were there. They paused in their talk to admire her face and her grace, and they thought, "This must be the governor's daughter!" They brought her sherbet and cakes made with almonds and honey and they sat her in the place of honor in the middle of them all. She looked for her step-mother with her daughter and saw them far off, near the door where the peasants were sitting, and the wives of weavers and peddlers.

Her stepmother stared at her and said to herself, "O Allah Whom we praise, how much this lady resembles my husband's daughter! But then, don't they say, 'Every seven men were made from one clod of clay?'" And the stepmother never knew that it was her very own husband's daughter and none other!

Not to spin out our tale, before the rest of the women stood up, the fisherman's daughter went to the mother of the bride to say, "May it be with God's blessings and bounty, O my aunt!" and hurried out. The sun had set and darkness was falling. On her way the girl had to cross a bridge over the stream that flowed into the king's gar-den. And by fate and divine decree, it happened that as she ran over the bridge one of her golden clogs fell off her foot and into the river below. It was too far to climb down to the water and search in the dusk; what if her stepmother should return home before her? So the girl took off her other shoe, and pulling her cloak around her head, dashed on her way.

When she reached the house she shucked her fine clothes, rolled the pearly comb and golden clog inside them, and hid them under the woodpile. She rubbed her head and hands and feet with earth to make them dirty, and she was standing with her broom when her stepmother found her. The wife looked into her face and exam-ined her hands and feet and said, "Still sweeping after sunset? Or are you hoping to sweep our lives away?"

What of the golden clog? Well, the current carried it into the king's garden and rolled it and rolled it until it came to rest in the pool where the king's son led his stal-lion to drink. Next day the prince was watering the horse. He saw that every time it lowered its head to drink, something made it shy and step back. What could there be at the bottom of the pool to frighten his stallion? He called the groom, and from the mud the man brought him the shining clog of gold.

When the prince held the beautiful little thing in his hand, he began to imagine the beautiful little foot that had worn it. He walked back to the palace with his heart busy and his mind full of the girl who owned so precious a shoe. The queen saw him lost in thought and said, "May Allah send us good news; why so careworn, my son?" "Yammah, Mother, I want you to find me a wife!" said the prince. "So much thought over one wife and no more?" said the queen. "I'll find you a thousand if you wish! I'll bring every girl in the kingdom to be your wife if you want! But tell me, my son, who is the girl who has stolen your reason?" "I want to marry the girl who owns this clog," replied the prince, and he told his mother how he had found it. "You shall have her, my son," said the queen. "I shall begin my search tomorrow as soon as it is light, and I shall not stop till I find her."

The very next day the prince's mother went to work, in at one house and out at the next with the golden clog tucked under her arm. Wherever she saw a young woman, she measured the shoe against the sole of the maiden's foot. Meanwhile the prince sat in the palace gate waiting for her return. "What news, Mother?" he asked. And she said, "Nothing yet, my son. Be patient, child, put snow on your breast and cool your passion. I'll find her yet."

And so the search continued. Entering at one gate and leaving at the next, the queen visited the houses of the nobles and the merchants and the goldsmiths. She saw the daughters of the craftsmen and the tradesmen. She went into the huts of the water carriers and the weavers, and stopped at each house until only the fishermen's hovels on the bank of the river were left. Every evening when the prince asked for news, she said, "I'll find her, I'll find her."

When the fisherfolk were told that the queen was coming to visit their houses, that wily fisherman's wife got busy. She bathed her daughter and dressed her in her best, she rinsed her hair with henna and rimmed her eyes with *kohl* and rubbed her cheeks till they glowed red. But still when the girl stood beside the fisherman's daughter, it was like a candle in the sun. Much as the stepchild had been ill-treated and starved, through the will of Allah and with the help of the little red fish, she had grown in beauty from day to day. Now her stepmother dragged her out of the house and into the yard. She pushed her into the bakehouse and covered its mouth with the round clay tray on which she spread her dough. This she held down with the stone of her handmill. "Don't dare move until I come for you!" said the stepmother. What could the poor girl do but crouch in the ashes and trust in Allah to save her?

When the queen arrived the stepmother pushed her daughter forward, saying, "Kiss the hands of the prince's mother, ignorant child!" As she had done in the other houses, the queen set the girl beside her and held up her foot and measured the golden clog against it. Just at that moment the neighbor's rooster flew into the yard and began to crow,

> Ki-ki-ki-kow!
> Let the king's wife know
> They put the ugly one on show
> And hid the beauty down below!
> Ki-ki-ki-kow!

He began again with his piercing cry, and the stepmother raced out and flapped her arms to chase him away. But the queen had heard the words, and she sent her servants to search both high and low. When they pushed aside the cover off the mouth of the oven, they found the girl—fair as the moon in the midst of the ashes. They brought her to the queen, and the golden clog fit as if it had been the mold from which her foot was cast.

The queen was satisfied. She said, "From this hour that daughter of yours is betrothed to my son. Make ready for the wedding. God willing, the procession shall come for her on Friday." And she gave the stepmother a purse filled with gold.

When the woman realized that her plans had failed, that her husband's daughter was to marry the prince while her own remained in the house, she was filled with anger and rage. "I'll see that he sends her back before the night is out," she said.

She took the purse of gold, ran to the perfumer's bazaar, and asked for a purge so strong that it would shred the bowels to tatters. At the sight of the gold the perfumer began to mix the powders in his tray. Then she asked for arsenic and lime, which weaken hair and make it fall, and an ointment that smelled like carrion.

Now the stepmother prepared the bride for her wedding. She washed her hair with henna mixed with arsenic and lime, and spread the foul ointment over her hair. Then she held the girl by her ear and poured the purge down her throat. Soon the wedding procession arrived, with horses and drums, fluttering bright clothes, and the sounds of jollity. They lifted the bride onto the litter and took her away. She came to the palace preceded by music and followed by singing and chanting and clapping of hands. She entered the chamber, the prince lifted the veil off her face, and she shone like a fourteen-day moon. A scent of amber and roses made the prince press his face to her hair. He ran his fingers over her locks, and it was like a man playing with cloth of gold. Now the bride began to feel a heaviness in her belly, but from under the hem of her gown there fell gold pieces in thousands till the carpet and the cushions were covered with gold.

Meanwhile the stepmother waited in her doorway, saying, "Now they'll bring her back in disgrace. Now she'll come home all filthy and bald." But though she stood in the doorway till dawn, from the palace no one came.

The news of the prince's fair wife began to fill the town, and the master merchant's son said to his mother, "They say that the prince's bride has a sister. I want her for my bride." Going to the fisherman's hut, his mother gave the fisherman's wife a purse full of gold and said, "Prepare the bride, for we shall come for her on Friday if God wills." And the fisherman's wife said to herself, "If what I did for my husband's daughter turned her hair to threads of gold and her belly to a fountain of coins, shall I not do the same for my own child?" She hastened to the perfumer and asked for the same powders and drugs, but stronger than before. Then she prepared her child, and the wedding procession came. When the merchant's son lifted her veil, it was like lifting the cover off a grave. The stink was so strong that it choked him, and her hair came away in his hands. So they wrapped the poor bride in her own filth and carried her back to her mother.

As for the prince, he lived with the fisherman's daughter in great happiness and joy, and God blessed them with seven children like seven golden birds.

Mulberry, mulberry,
So ends my story.
If my house were not so far
I'd bring you figs and raisins in a jar.

THE INDIAN CINDERELLA[1]

Cyrus Macmillan

ON THE SHORES OF A wide bay on the Atlantic coast there dwelt in old times a great Indian warrior. It was said that he had been one of Glooskap's best helpers and friends, and that he had done for him many wonderful deeds. But that, no man knows. He had, however, a very wonderful and strange power; he could make himself invisible; he could thus mingle unseen with his enemies and listen to their plots. He was known among the people as Strong Wind, the Invisible. He dwelt with his sister in a tent near the sea, and his sister helped him greatly in his work. Many maidens would have been glad to marry him, and he was much sought after because of his mighty deeds; and it was known that Strong Wind would marry the first maiden who could see him as he came home at night. Many made the trial, but it was a long time before one succeeded.

Strong Wind used a clever trick to test the truthfulness of all who sought to win him. Each evening as the day went down, his sister walked on the beach with any girl who wished to make the trial. His sister could always see him, but no one else could see him. And as he came home from work in the twilight, his sister as she saw him drawing near would ask the girl who sought him, "Do you see him?" And each girl would falsely answer, "Yes." And his sister would ask, "With what does he draw his sled?" And each girl would answer, "With the hide of a moose," or "With a pole," or "With a great cord." And then his sister would know that they all had lied, for their answers were mere guesses. And many tried and lied and failed, for Strong Wind would not marry any who were untruthful.

There lived in the village a great chief who had three daughters. Their mother had been long dead. One of these was much younger than the others. She was very

1   From *Canadian Wonder Tales* (London: John Lane, the Bodley Head, 1918).

beautiful and gentle and well beloved by all, and for that reason her older sisters were very jealous of her charms and treated her very cruelly. They clothed her in rags that she might be ugly; and they cut off her long black hair; and they burned her face with coals from the fire that she might be scarred and disfigured. And they lied to their father, telling him that she had done these things herself. But the young girl was patient and kept her gentle heart and went gladly about her work.

Like other girls, the chief's two eldest daughters tried to win Strong Wind. One evening, as the day went down, they walked on the shore with Strong Wind's sister and waited for his coming. Soon he came home from his day's work, drawing his sled. And his sister asked as usual, "Do you see him?" And each one, lying, answered, "Yes." And she asked, "Of what is his shoulder strap made?" And each, guessing, said, "Of rawhide." Then they entered the tent where they hoped to see Strong Wind eating his supper; and when he took off his coat and his moccasins they could see them, but more than these they saw nothing. And Strong Wind knew that they had lied, and he kept himself from their sight, and they went home dismayed.

One day the chief's youngest daughter with her rags and her burnt face resolved to seek Strong Wind. She patched her clothes with bits of birch bark from the trees, and put on the few little ornaments she possessed, and went forth to try to see the Invisible One as all the other girls of the village had done before. And her sisters laughed at her and called her "Fool"; and as she passed along the road all the people laughed at her because of her tattered frock and her burnt face, but silently she went her way.

Strong Wind's sister received the little girl kindly, and at twilight she took her to the beach. Soon Strong Wind came home drawing his sled. And his sister asked, "Do you see him?" And the girl answered, "No," and his sister wondered greatly because she spoke the truth. And again she asked, "Do you see him now?" And the girl answered, "Yes, and he is very wonderful." And she asked, "With what does he draw his sled?" And the girl answered, "With the Rainbow," and she was much afraid. And she asked further, "Of what is his bowstring?" And the girl answered, "His bowstring is the Milky Way."

Then Strong Wind's sister knew that because the girl had spoken the truth at first her brother had made himself visible to her. And she said, "Truly, you have seen him." And she took her home and bathed her, and all the scars disappeared from her face and body; and her hair grew long and black again like the raven's wing; and she gave her fine clothes to wear and many rich ornaments. Then she bade her take the wife's seat in the tent. Soon Strong Wind entered and sat beside her, and called her his bride. The very next day she became his wife, and ever afterwards she helped him to do great deeds. The girl's two elder sisters were very cross, and they wondered greatly at what had taken place. But Strong Wind, who knew of their cruelty, resolved to punish them. Using his great power, he changed them both into aspen trees and rooted them in the earth. And since that day the leaves of the aspen have always trembled, and they shiver in fear at the approach of Strong Wind, it matters not how softly he comes, for they are still mindful of his great power and anger because of their lies and their cruelty to their sister long ago.

GROWING UP (IS HARD TO DO)

As we have seen, the fairy tale did not begin life as the exclusive property of children, for the simple reason that it was originally told by and for adults—which explains what many would now consider its occasionally unsuitable subject matter. We must remember that the concept of childhood has only emerged over the last three to four hundred years; in earlier times, childhood was simply not perceived as being a distinct entity. The explanation for this is partly economic and partly psychological in nature. Among the peasantry, children represented a natural resource, but of a kind that required years of nurturing before any return could be expected—years during which the child was actually a drain on scarce resources, with no guarantee that he or she would live long enough to repay such an investment. The child was obliged to grow up quickly and fend for him or herself, so in a world where mere survival was so constant a challenge, it is reasonable to speculate that the emotional attachment between parent and child was sometimes less intense than in our own world of relative affluence and leisure. Their social and psychological insignificance make it all the more surprising that children are as well-represented in the fairy tale as they are. However, the point must be made that although many of the tales we have read so far *begin* with childhood, their major emphasis is upon the transition to adulthood. The tales in this section are distinguished by the fact that their focus is specifically upon childhood, with little or no reference to later life.

There is a deep-seated ambivalence toward children reflected in fairy tales. These tales are about children not so much because they are perceived as interesting or entertaining characters (as is generally the assumption today) but rather as representatives of the upcoming generation, prospective claimants of adult privilege and status. On the one hand, there are tales in which love and protectiveness toward offspring are expressed—more often, it may be added, in tales about the rich than about the poor—although the overprotectiveness found in such tales as "Little Red Riding Hood," "Sleeping Beauty," and now "Rapunzel" can be seen as leading to unhappy consequences. On the other hand, there is fear and resentment of the child as a potential rival, memorably depicted in "Snow White."

But why is it that so many of the "classic" fairy tales focus upon the girl? The answer, at least in part, is that it has long been more of a challenge to grow up female than to grow up male. The inequality of the sexes runs as a central thread through tale after tale, although there is sometimes an intriguing contrast between the conventional role and the actual behavior of some heroines. One distinction is worthy of note: while the princesses we have encountered thus far all manifest differing degrees of passivity, the peasant girls, such as Gretel or the unnamed girl in "The Story of Grandmother," seem to be much more willing and able to seize the initiative. Is this another indication of how important class is in determining patterns of behavior? Yet given the centuries of social prejudice through which these stories have been filtered, these patterns should not surprise us too much. We were well into the second half of the twentieth century, in fact, before serious efforts were made (in the form of the feminist fairy tale) to challenge the assumptions that are firmly entrenched in many traditional tales. Quite apart from the innate originality and inventiveness of the narratives themselves, the popular success of such tales as "Sleeping Beauty," "Cinderella," and "Snow White" has been equally attributable to the preconceptions and values of nineteenth-century readers—and fairy-tale collectors.

Curiously enough, the few male children who have gained an equivalent renown are either disadvantaged by their small size (like Hop o' my Thumb) or else delinquent ne'er-do-wells such as Jack (of beanstalk fame) or even Aladdin from *The Arabian Nights*. The point here, of course, is that out of such unpromising beginnings comes a winner, through the exercise of such "masculine" qualities as courage, audacity, determination, and a measure of ruthlessness.

The similarities between Perrault's "Hop o' my Thumb" and the Grimms' "Hansel and Gretel" are of course striking (yet another version of the tale is to be found in Basile's *Pentamerone*). A careful comparison of these tales illuminates some of the intriguing differences in social values and attitudes between the aristocratic Perrault and the more bourgeois Grimms. In his influential essay "On Fairy Stories," J.R.R. Tolkien uses the apt metaphor of the "Cauldron of Stories" to suggest the constantly-replenished mixture of plot, character, and setting that produces the fairy tale; there is some flavor of the cauldron in "Hop o' my Thumb," in its dash of "Jack and the Beanstalk," its soupçon of "Cinderella" ...

The presence and power of the mother is very much an issue in four of the tales in this section; in both "Hansel and Gretel" and "Snow White," the Grimms chose in later editions to turn mother into stepmother, no doubt because they did not wish to confront their child-readers with such unnatural maternal behavior. (Although the witch in "Rapunzel" has no family connection with the girl, she nevertheless represents another example of the "bad mother.") By contrast, the father is either entirely absent or a subservient figure.

Several of these tales begin with a depiction of physical hardship—and that is surely based in historical fact. Poverty and famine are experiences that few of us have suffered at first hand, and so we have little conception of the profound effects they have on those afflicted. So while we may brand the mother of Hansel and Gretel as cold-hearted and cruel, we cannot deny that she is responding to a harsh reality in a pragmatic fashion. Is it possible that the roots of these tales reach back to a time when children were, in such extreme circumstances, seen as expendable? In "Jack and the Beanstalk," the situation is reversed, with the widowed mother at the mercy of her immature, good-for-nothing son; while there is certainly no evil intent here, the prospect is nevertheless the same—imminent starvation.

The similarity of structure continues into the second phase of the tales, wherein the realistic gives way to the fantastic, and the child-characters must learn to fend for themselves or perish in the attempt. That they succeed in overcoming the adult characters who oppose them should be seen as a practical acknowledgment of the way the world works, rather than as a glorification of intrepid youth. Any notion of the child as natural adventurer and hero was simply incompatible with the attitudes toward childhood that prevailed in earlier times.

Not surprisingly, Freudian critics such as Bruno Bettelheim have much to say about these visceral conflicts between child and adult which, by virtue of being played out in the realm of the imaginary, sublimate anxiety-creating aggression and rivalry into a form that the listener/reader can accept and resolve. Hansel and Gretel return home (escaping the fantasy world via an obviously symbolic body of water) to discover that their stepmother has died in their absence. The link between mother and witch seems obvious, and although the children choose to return home, one senses that they are now more likely to look after their father, rather than the reverse. Thanks in part to the intervention of the dwarves, Snow White survives repeated attempts on her life by her rival (step)mother and after a Sleeping Beauty-style period of growth, emerges as a woman from her coffin-cocoon. It is Rapunzel who arguably suffers the most in the transition from childhood to adulthood—perhaps because her experience is explicitly sexual.

For his part, Jack comes back to earth the same way he left, but as a dramatically different person—the Jack who kills the giant and bestows wealth and security upon his mother is no longer an aimless, impulsive boy. We must, however, confront the moral question that arises from Jack's thefts from the giant, the last of which seems particularly gratuitous, in that his wealth is assured by his possession of the hen that lays the golden eggs. Some versions of this tale present it as a matter of revenge: Jack's father is absent from the story because he has been killed by the giant, and so

Jack is simply reclaiming his own. In the case of *this* version, the explanation must be that we judge motive according to the folk tale's simple—even primitive—moral code: the giant is by nature wicked (as his earlier behavior has amply revealed) and, therefore, his possessions must be ill-gotten. If Jack has the youthful audacity to make the attempt, then to the victor go the spoils. The new generation has passed the test and takes its rightful place—until it in turn finds itself cast in the role of giant or witch, and the struggle begins anew …

The final tale in this section stands apart from the others but is unquestionably about growing up—to the extent that its title has entered the language as a description of childhood experience. "The Ugly Duckling," a paradigm of autobiographical fantasy, is arguably Hans Christian Andersen's most famous tale, recounting his struggle to extract himself from the poverty-stricken obscurity of his early years and to make his mark in the artistic world. It is as personal a statement as the others are generalized, reflecting an important difference between the anonymous folk tale and the literary tale—but part of Andersen's genius was in his ability to express everyone's experience in his own: all those feelings of inadequacy, rejection, and loneliness that we suffered (or *imagine* that we suffered) are captured in that single unforgettable image of the duckling.

HOP O' MY THUMB[1]

Charles Perrault

A CERTAIN WOODCUTTER AND HIS WIFE were blessed with seven sons. The eldest was ten years old and the youngest seven. It may seem a remarkable feat to produce so many children in so little time but the woodcutter's wife had gone to work with a will and rarely given her husband less than two at once.

They were very poor and their seven children were a great inconvenience because none of them could earn their living.

The youngest was the greatest inconvenience of all; he was a weakling and a mute, and they mistook his debility for stupidity. He was very, very tiny and when he came into the world he was scarcely bigger than your thumb. So they called him "Hop o' my Thumb."

This poor child was the butt of the household and they were always finding fault

---

1   First published in 1697. This text from *Sleeping Beauty and Other Favourite Fairy Tales*, trans. Angela Carter (London: Gollancz, 1982).

with him. But he was really the cleverest of them all and if he did not speak much, he listened very, very carefully.

At last there came a year of such terrible famine that the poor people decided they could not provide for their children any more.

One evening, when the children were in bed and the woodcutter sat with his wife by the fire, he said to her with a breaking heart:

"You know we've got nothing to give our children to eat. I can't bear to see them die of hunger in front of my very eyes. I've decided to take them out in the woods to-morrow and lose them there. It will be very easy. While they are gathering up sticks, we'll slip away without them seeing us."

"Oh!" cried his wife. "How could you think of abandoning your own children?"

Her husband painted her a grisly picture of their plight but, all the same, she would not agree to his scheme—she was poor, but she was their mother. But then when she thought how sad she would be to see them starve to death, she said, yes; and went to bed in tears.

When Hop o' my Thumb had realised his parents were discussing something of importance, he crept from his bed and hid himself under his father's stool, to eavesdrop, so he heard everything they said. Back he went to bed but he did not sleep that night; he was planning his strategy. He got up early and went to the bank of a stream, and filled his pockets with little white pebbles. Then he came home again. When the family set off for the wood, Hop o' my Thumb did not tell his brothers his dreadful secret.

They went to the thickest part of the forest, where you could not see another person if you were ten steps away from them. The woodcutter began to chop down a tree and the children went off to collect sticks and make them up into bundles. When their father and mother saw they were busy and happy, they edged further and further away, until they could no longer glimpse a single child: then they took to their heels and fled.

When the children found out they were all by themselves, they began to cry with all their might. Hop o' my Thumb let them cry for a while, because he knew how to get back home again. As they walked through the forest, he had let drop the little white pebbles he had kept in his pocket all along the way. Now he said to his brothers:

"Don't be scared. Mother and father have abandoned us here, but I will take you home again. Just follow me."

They trooped after him and he led them straight home by the same way they had gone into the forest. At first, they did not dare go inside the cottage, but listened at the door to find out what was going on.

As soon as the woodcutter and his wife had arrived home, the village squire sent them ten golden sovereigns he had owed them for so long they had given up hope he would ever repay the debt. The money was life to them; they were dying of hunger. The woodcutter sent his wife straight out to the butcher's. They had not eaten for so long she had forgotten how much meat to buy and bought three times as much as the two of them needed. When they sat down at the table, the woodcutter's wife lamented:

"Alas, where are our poor children now? They would have feasted off the leavings of our spread! But you would insist in getting rid of them, William; I told you we would regret it. What are they doing in the forest? Perhaps the wolves have already eaten them! What an inhuman brute you are, to abandon your children!"

If she reminded him once she reminded him twenty times how he'd regret it and at last he lost patience with her and threatened to beat her if she did not keep quiet. She was making a deafening clamour and he was the kind of man who likes a woman to speak her mind but can't stand a woman who is always right.

The woodcutter's wife was crying dreadfully.

"Alas, alas, where are my poor children?"

She cried so loudly that the children outside heard her and sang out all together: "Here we are! Here we are!"

She ran to open the door for them and hugged and kissed them.

"Oh, my darlings, how happy I am to see you! You must be very tired, you must be very hungry … Oh, Pierrot! How dirty you are! Come and have your face washed!"

Pierrot was her eldest son and she loved him more than all the others because he had ginger hair and her own hair was on the carroty side, too.

They sat down and ate so much their mother and father were filled with joy. They told their parents how scary the forest had been, interrupting one another and all talking at once. The woodcutter and his wife were delighted to have their children home with them and the joy lasted exactly as long as the ten golden sovereigns. But when the money was all gone, they began to despair and decided, once again, to leave the children to their fates. But this time there would be no mistake. They would take the children twice as far from home before they abandoned them, so they could never return.

But they could not plot secretly enough to stop Hop o' my Thumb hearing them and he made it his business to organise things as he had done before. But when he got up at dawn to go and fetch his pebbles, his scheme came to nothing, for he found the door of the house securely locked. He did not know what to do until the wood-cutter's wife gave each of them a piece of bread for their lunch.

Then he thought he would be able to use breadcrumbs instead of pebbles to scatter behind him along the way, so he stored his bread in his pocket.

Their father and mother took them to the densest, darkest part of the forest and once they had arrived, they slipped away through the undergrowth and left the children behind. Hop o' my Thumb did not worry very much, at first, because he thought he could easily find his way home because of the track of breadcrumbs he had scattered as he walked; but he was astonished to discover he could not find a single crumb when he started to look for them, because the birds had come and eaten them all.

Now they were in a sorry state. The more they searched for the way home, the more they lost themselves in the forest. Night came on and brought a great wind with it, so they were very much afraid. They thought they heard the howling of wolves who had come to devour them. They hardly dared speak. Then it began to rain and they were soaked through. They slithered in the mud at every step, fell down and dragged themselves to their feet again, filthy from head to toe.

Hop o' my Thumb climbed up a tree to see if he could discover anything about their surroundings. He looked about on all sides until he saw a little glimmer of light like the light from a candle, far off in the forest. When he came down from his perch, he could see nothing but he made his brothers trudge off in the direction of the light and, after a while, they saw it again as they came out of the wood.

At last they arrived at the house with the candle in the window, not without more alarms—they often lost sight of the light and fell into holes several times. They knocked at the door and a woman answered it. She asked them what they wanted.

"We are poor children lost in the forest," replied Hop o' my Thumb. "Can we beg a bed for the night, in the name of charity?"

The woman saw how pretty they were and began to weep.

"Oh, you poor children, why have you come? Don't you know who lives here? A horrid ogre, who eats babies."

Hop o' my Thumb shook with fear, like his brothers, but he said:

"Oh, kind lady, what shall we do? If you don't let us into your house, the wolves in the forest will certainly eat us. And on the whole, we would very much rather be eaten by the ogre than by the wolves, because the ogre might take pity on us, especially if you ask him to."

The ogre's wife thought she would be able to hide them until the next morning, so she let them in and took them to warm themselves beside a good fire where a whole sheep was turning on a spit for the ogre's supper.

While they were thawing out, they heard three or four great bangs at the door; the ogre had come home. The ogre's wife hid them under the bed and went to let him in. The ogre asked if his supper was ready and his wine drawn from the barrel; then he sat down at the table. The sheep was still turning on the spit but he thought he smelled something better than roast mutton. He snuffed the air to the right and he snuffed the air to the left; he said he smelled fresh meat.

"Why, that must be the calf I was just going to skin!" said his wife.

"I smell fresh meat, I tell you," repeated the ogre, looking at his wife suspiciously. "And something is going on that I don't understand."

He got up and went straight to the bed.

"So you wanted to trick me, did you, you old cow! I don't know why I don't eat you, too, but I daresay you'd be too tough. Here's some game delivered to me at just the right time—the very thing to give my three ogrish friends for dinner tomorrow!"

One after the other, he pulled the poor children from under the bed. They fell to their knees and begged his pardon but they had fallen into the hands of the cruellest of ogres, who, far from taking pity on them, was already eating them up with his eyes and telling his wife they were such delicious morsels that she would have to make an especially good sauce to go with them.

He got out an enormous knife and began to sharpen it on a long stone, under the terrified gaze of Hop o' my Thumb and his brothers. But when he seized hold of Pierrot, his wife said:

"What can you be thinking of, slaughtering at this hour? Won't there be enough time tomorrow?"

"Keep your mouth shut," said the ogre. "I like my game well hung."

"But goodness me, isn't there enough meat in the house already? There's a calf, two sheep and the best part of a pig."

"Oh, very well, then," said the ogre. "Give them some supper to fatten them up and put them to bed."

The ogre's wife was overjoyed and took them plenty of supper but they were too frightened to eat it. As for the ogre, he sat down to some serious drinking to celebrate his pleasure at finding such delicious fare with which to entertain his friends. He put away twice as much good wine as usual and it went to his head, so he stretched out on his bed for a nap.

The ogre had seven little daughters who all had wonderfully fresh complexions because they ate so much fresh meat, just like their father. But besides their rosy cheeks, they had nasty little round grey eyes, hooked noses and enormous mouths with long green teeth sharpened to a point, and those teeth had huge gaps between them. They were still too young to be very wicked but they showed signs of great promise and had already taken to biting babies in order to suck their blood.

The horrid little things had all been sent to bed early and were lying, all seven, in one bed, and each wore a golden crown on her head. There was another bed just the same size in their room and the ogre's wife put the seven boys to sleep in it before she went to lie down beside her husband.

Hop o' my Thumb saw the golden crowns on the heads of the little ogresses. He was afraid the ogre might wake up in the night and want to get on with his butchering; after a while, Hop o' my Thumb got up and took the caps off the heads of his brothers. He crept across the room and took the crowns from the heads of the baby ogresses. He put the crowns on his brothers' heads and one on his own, and put their caps on the baby ogresses, so that the ogre would think the woodcutter's sons were his own daughters and the girls were really the boys.

About midnight, the ogre woke up and was seized with regret that he had left till the morrow a task he might have performed that day. He jumped out of bed and picked up his big knife.

"Let's go and have another look at those funny little objects," he said to himself.

He tiptoed into his daughters' bedroom and went to the bed where the little boys slept soundly, except for Hop o' my Thumb, who was very frightened when the ogre's hands groped at his face. But when the ogre touched the golden crown he wore, he said:

"Why, what a nasty trick I almost played on myself! I must have had a drop too much last night."

So off he went to the other bed and felt for the boys' caps.

"Here they are, the little lambs!" he cried. "Let's fall to work."

With that, he slit the throats of his seven daughters. Well content with the night's work, he went back to bed again.

As soon as Hop o' my Thumb heard the ogre start to snore, he woke up his brothers and told them to put their clothes on and follow him. They went into the garden as quietly as they could and jumped over the wall. Shaking with terror, they ran through the night without even knowing where they were going.

When the ogre woke up in the morning, he said to his wife:

"Go down below and get those little fellows from last night ready."

The ogre's wife was surprised and pleased because she thought he meant "get them ready for the day," not "get them ready for the pot." She thought he had taken pity on them. So upstairs she went, and found her seven daughters, with their throats cut, swimming in blood.

She responded with a fainting fit; most women faint in similar circumstances. The ogre thought his wife had been away long enough and climbed up the stairs to see what the matter was. He was no less astonished than his wife at the spectacle which awaited him.

"What have I done?" he cried. "I'll pay the rascals back for the trick they played me, and pay them back quickly!"

He threw a bucket of water over his wife to bring her round and when she came to he said:

"Quick, get me my seven-league boots so that I can go and catch those criminals!"

He raced across the country until he came to the lane where the poor children were running, and now they were only a hundred yards from their own father's door.

They saw the ogre striding from mountain to mountain, and skipping across rivers as if they were streams. Hop o' my Thumb spied a crack in a nearby rock and quickly hid his six brothers there. He tucked himself in beside them, peering out to keep an eye on the ogre. The ogre was weary after his long, useless search; besides, seven-league boots are very exhausting to wear. He wanted a sit down and, as luck would have it, he parked himself on the very rock in which the little boys were hiding.

He was so tired that soon he fell asleep and began to snore so frightfully that the poor children were just as frightened as they had been when be was flourishing his big knife ready to cut their throats. But Hop o' my Thumb told his brothers to run home while the giant was sound asleep and not to bother about him, because he could take care of himself. So off they ran.

Hop o' my Thumb went up to the ogre, took the boots off his feet so gently he did not wake him, and put them on himself. The boots were very long and very large but, since they were of fairy make, they could swell or shrink according to the size of the foot that wore them.

Hop o' my Thumb went to the ogre's house straight away. The ogre's wife was weeping beside the corpses of her daughters.

"Your husband is in terrible danger," announced Hop o' my Thumb. "He has been captured by a gang of robbers who say they will kill him if he doesn't give them all his money. As they held the knife to his throat, he noticed me standing discreetly by and begged me to come straight to you and tell you to give me everything he owns and not keep back a penny. Otherwise, the robbers will kill him without mercy. He told me to borrow his seven-league boots because the matter was so pressing, and to prove to you I was no imposter, too."

The good woman was terrified and quickly gave him all she had, because the ogre was a good husband in spite of his daily diet of young children, and she wanted to save him. Hop o' my Thumb, loaded with the ogre's treasure, took himself off to his father's house, where he had the most joyful welcome.

Some people disagree with this ending—they say that Hop o' my Thumb never robbed the ogre and the truth of it was, that he only took the seven-league boots. These people claim they know the true facts and, to clinch the matter, go so far as to say they have even enjoyed the hospitality of the woodcutter's own home. They say that when Hop o' my Thumb put on the ogre's boots, he went to the king's court because he knew an enemy army was camped two miles away and all at the capital were agog to know the results of the latest battle. They say he went to the king and asked him if he wanted full military reports before sunset. The king promised him a great deal of money for the information and Hop o' my Thumb brought back the news that very evening. After that, the king paid him handsomely to carry orders to the army; besides, a great many ladies paid him any price he cared to name for news of their lovers. He made his greatest profits from this activity.

One or two married women also hired him to send letters to their husbands but they paid very badly and provided very little business; it was a poor thing in comparison.

He worked as a special messenger until he saved up a small fortune. Then he went home to his father's house. He took good care of his entire family; he bought peerages for his father and all his brothers and lived in ease and comfort for the rest of his life.

Moral

It is no affliction to have a large family if they are all handsome, strong and clever. But if one of them is a puny weakling, he will be despised, jeered at and mocked. However, often the runt of the litter ends up making the family fortune.

HANSEL AND GRETEL[1]

Jacob and Wilhelm Grimm

AT THE EDGE OF A large forest there lived a poor woodcutter with his wife and two children. The little boy's name was Hansel, and the little girl's was Gretel. There was never much to eat in the house, and once, in time of famine, there wasn't even enough bread to go around. One night the woodcutter lay in bed thinking, tossing and turning with worry. All at once he sighed and said to his wife: "What's to become of us? How can we feed our poor children when we haven't even got enough for ourselves?" His wife answered: "Husband, listen to me. Tomorrow at daybreak we'll take the children out to the thickest part of the forest and make a fire for them and give them each a piece of bread. Then we'll leave them and go about our work. They'll never find the way home again and that way we'll be rid of them." "No, Wife," said the man. "I won't do it. How can I bring myself to leave my children alone in the woods? The wild beasts will come and tear them to pieces." "You fool!" she said. "Then all four of us will starve. You may as well start planing the boards for our coffins." And she gave him no peace until he consented. "But I still feel badly about the poor children," he said.

The children were too hungry to sleep, and they heard what their stepmother said to their father. Gretel wept bitter tears and said: "Oh, Hansel, we're lost." "Hush,

---

1 First published in 1812/15, in the first edition of *Kinder- und Hausmärchen*. This text from the second edition (1819), from *Grimms' Tales for Young and Old*, trans. Ralph Manheim (Garden City, NY: Anchor P, 1977).

Gretel," said Hansel. "Don't worry. I'll find a way." When the old people had fallen asleep, he got up, put on his little jacket, opened the bottom half of the Dutch door, and crept outside. The moon was shining bright, and the pebbles around the house glittered like silver coins. Hansel crouched down and stuffed his pocket full of them. Then he went back and said to Gretel: "Don't worry, little sister. Just go to sleep, God won't forsake us," and went back to bed.

At daybreak, before the sun had risen, the woman came and woke the two children. "Get up, you lazybones. We're going to the forest for wood." Then she gave each a piece of bread and said: "This is for your noonday meal. Don't eat it too soon, because there won't be any more." Gretel put the bread under her apron, because Hansel had pebbles in his pocket. Then they all started out for the forest together. When they had gone a little way, Hansel stopped still and looked back in the direction of their house, and every so often he did it again. His father said: "Hansel, why do you keep looking back and lagging behind? Wake up and don't forget what your legs are for." "Oh, father," said Hansel, "I'm looking for my white kitten; he's sitting on the roof, trying to bid me good-bye." The woman said: "You fool, that's not your white kitten. It's the morning sun shining on the chimney." But Hansel hadn't been looking at his kitten. Each time, he had taken a shiny pebble from his pocket and dropped it on the ground.

When they came to the middle of the forest, the father said: "Start gathering wood, children, and I'll make a fire to keep you warm." Hansel and Gretel gathered brushwood till they had a little pile of it. The brushwood was kindled and when the flames were high enough the woman said: "Now, children, lie down by the fire and rest. We're going into the forest to cut wood. When we're done, we'll come back and get you."

Hansel and Gretel sat by the fire, and at midday they both ate their pieces of bread. They heard the strokes of an ax and thought their father was nearby. But it wasn't an ax, it was a branch he had tied to a withered tree, and the wind was shaking it to and fro. After sitting there for some time, they became so tired that their eyes closed and they fell into a deep sleep. When at last they awoke, it was dark night. Gretel began to cry and said: "How will we ever get out of this forest?" But Hansel comforted her: "Just wait a little while. As soon as the moon rises, we'll find the way." And when the full moon had risen, Hansel took his little sister by the hand and followed the pebbles, which glistened like newly minted silver pieces and showed them the way. They walked all night and reached their father's house just as day was breaking. They knocked at the door, and when the woman opened it and saw Hansel and Gretel, she said: "Wicked children! Why did you sleep so long in the forest? We thought you'd never get home." But their father was glad, for he had been very unhappy about deserting them.

A while later the whole country was again stricken with famine, and the children

GROWING UP (IS HARD TO DO)

heard their mother[1] talking to their father in bed at night: "Everything has been eaten up. We still have half a loaf of bread, and when that's gone there will be no more. The children must go. We'll take them still deeper into the forest, and this time they won't find their way home; it's our only hope." The husband was heavy-hearted, and he thought: "It would be better if I shared the last bite with my children." But the woman wouldn't listen to anything he said; she only scolded and found fault. Once you've said yes, it's hard to say no, and so it was that the woodcutter gave in again.

But the children were awake; they had heard the conversation. When the old people had fallen asleep, Hansel got up again. He wanted to pick up some more pebbles, but the woman had locked the door and he couldn't get out. But he comforted his little sister and said: "Don't cry, Gretel. Just go to sleep, God will help us."

Early in the morning the woman came and got the children out of bed. She gave them their pieces of bread, but they were smaller than the last time. On the way to the forest, Hansel crumbled his bread in his pocket. From time to time he stopped and dropped a few crumbs on the ground. "Hansel," said his father, "why are you always stopping and looking back? Keep moving." "I'm looking at my little pigeon," said Hansel. "He's sitting on the roof, trying to bid me good-bye." "Fool," said the woman. "That's not your little pigeon, it's the morning sun shining on the chimney." But little by little Hansel strewed all his bread on the ground.

The woman led the children still deeper into the forest, to a place where they had never been in all their lives. Again a big fire was made, and the mother said: "Just sit here, children. If you get tired, you can sleep awhile. We're going into the forest to cut wood, and this evening when we've finished we'll come and get you." At midday Gretel shared her bread with Hansel, who had strewn his on the ground. Then they fell asleep and the afternoon passed, but no one came for the poor children. It was dark night when they woke up, and Hansel comforted his little sister. "Gretel," he said, "just wait till the moon rises; then we'll see the breadcrumbs I strewed and they'll show us the way home." When the moon rose, they started out, but they didn't find any breadcrumbs, because the thousands of birds that fly around in the forests and fields had eaten them all up. Hansel said to Gretel: "Don't worry, we'll find the way," but they didn't find it. They walked all night and then all day from morning to night, but they were still in the forest, and they were very hungry, for they had nothing to eat but the few berries they could pick from the bushes. And when they were so tired their legs could carry them no farther, they lay down under a tree and fell asleep.

It was already the third morning since they had left their father's house. They started out again, but they were getting deeper and deeper into the forest, and unless

---

1   Mother: The Grimms were concerned that mothers in folk tales were often depicted as villains, so they made the editorial decision to transform them into stepmothers.

help came soon, they were sure to die of hunger and weariness. At midday, they saw a lovely snowbird sitting on a branch. It sang so beautifully that they stood still and listened. When it had done singing, it flapped its wings and flew on ahead, and they followed until the bird came to a little house and perched on the roof. When they came closer, they saw that the house was made of bread, and the roof was made of cake and the windows of sparkling sugar. "Let's eat," said Hansel, "and the Lord bless our food. I'll take a piece of the roof. You, Gretel, had better take some of the window; it's sweet." Hansel reached up and broke off a bit of the roof to see how it tasted, and Gretel pressed against the windowpanes and nibbled at them. And then a soft voice called from inside:

"Nibble nibble, little mouse,
  Who's that nibbling at my house?"

The children answered:

"The wind so wild,
  The heavenly child,"

and went right on eating. Hansel liked the taste of the roof, so he tore off a big chunk, and Gretel broke out a whole round windowpane and sat down on the ground to enjoy it. All at once the door opened, and an old, old woman with a crutch came hobbling out. Hansel and Gretel were so frightened they dropped what they were eating. But the old woman wagged her head and said: "Oh, what dear children! However did you get here? Don't be afraid, come in and stay with me. You will come to no harm." She took them by the hand and led them into her house. A fine meal of milk and pancakes, sugar, apples, and nuts was set before them. And then two little beds were made up clean and white, and Hansel and Gretel got into them and thought they were in heaven.

But the old woman had only pretended to be so kind. Actually she was a wicked witch, who waylaid children and had built her house out of bread to entice them. She killed, cooked, and ate any child who fell into her hands, and that to her was a feast day. Witches have red eyes and can't see very far, but they have a keen sense of smell like animals, so they know when humans are coming. As Hansel and Gretel approached, she laughed her wicked laugh and said with a jeer: "Here come two who will never get away from me." Early in the morning, when the children were still asleep, she got up, and when she saw them resting so sweetly with their plump red cheeks, she muttered to herself: "What tasty morsels they will be!" She grabbed Hansel with her scrawny hand, carried him to a little shed, and closed the iron-barred door behind him. He screamed for all he was worth, but much good it did him. Then she went back to Gretel, shook her awake, and cried: "Get up, lazybones. You must draw water and cook something nice for your brother. He's out in the shed and we've got to fatten him up. When he's nice and fat, I'm going to eat him." Gretel wept bitterly, but in vain; she had to do what the wicked witch told her.

The best of food was cooked for poor Hansel, but Gretel got nothing but crayfish shells. Every morning the old witch crept to the shed and said: "Hansel, hold out your finger. I want to see if you're getting fat." But Hansel held out a bone. The old woman had weak eyes and couldn't see it; she thought it was Hansel's finger and wondered why he wasn't getting fat. When four weeks had gone by and Hansel was as skinny as ever, her impatience got the better of her and she decided not to wait any longer. "Ho there, Gretel," she cried out. "Go and draw water and don't dawdle. Skinny or fat, I'm going to butcher Hansel tomorrow and cook him." Oh, how the little girl wailed at having to carry the water, and how the tears flowed down her cheeks! "Dear God," she cried, "oh, won't you help us? If only the wild beasts had eaten us in the forest, at least we'd have died together." "Stop that blubbering," said the witch. "It won't do you a bit of good."

Early in the morning Gretel had to fill the kettle with water and light the fire. "First we'll bake," said the old witch. "I've heated the oven and kneaded the dough." And she drove poor Gretel out to the oven, which by now was spitting flames. "Crawl in," said the witch, "and see if it's hot enough for the bread." Once Gretel was inside, she meant to close the door and roast her, so as to eat her too. But Gretel saw what she had in mind and said: "I don't know how. How do I get in?" "Silly goose," said the old woman. "The opening is big enough. Look. Even I can get in." She crept to the opening and stuck her head in, whereupon Gretel gave her a push that sent her sprawling, closed the iron door and fastened the bolt. Eek! How horribly she screeched! But Gretel ran away and the wicked witch burned miserably to death.

Gretel ran straight to Hansel, opened the door of the shed, and cried: "Hansel, we're saved! The old witch is dead." Hansel hopped out like a bird when someone opens the door of its cage. How happy they were! They hugged and kissed each other and danced around. And now that there was nothing to be afraid of, they went into the witch's house and in every corner there were boxes full of pearls and precious stones. Hansel stuffed his pockets full of them and said: "These will be much better than pebbles," and Gretel said: "I'll take some home too," and filled her apron with them. "We'd better leave now," said Hansel, "and get out of this bewitched forest." When they had walked a few hours, they came to a big body of water. "How will we ever get across," said Hansel. "I don't see any bridge." "And there's no boat, either," said Gretel, "but over there I see a white duck. She'll help us across if I ask her." And she cried out:

"Duckling, duckling, here is Gretel,
Duckling, duckling, here is Hansel,
No bridge or ferry far and wide—
Duckling, come and give us a ride."

Sure enough, the duck came over to them and Hansel sat down on her back and told his sister to sit beside him. "No," said Gretel, "that would be too much for the poor thing; let her carry us one at a time." And that's just what the good little duck did. And when they were safely across and had walked a little while, the forest began to look more and more familiar, and finally they saw their father's house in the distance. They began to run, and they flew into the house and threw themselves into their father's arms. The poor man hadn't had a happy hour since he had left the children in the forest, and in the meantime his wife had died. Gretel opened out her little apron, the pearls and precious stones went bouncing around the room, and Hansel reached into his pockets and tossed out handful after handful. All their worries were over, and they lived together in pure happiness. My story is done, see the mouse run; if you catch it, you may make yourself a great big fur cap out of it.

SNOW WHITE[1]

Jacob and Wilhelm Grimm

ONCE IN MIDWINTER WHEN THE snowflakes were falling from the sky like feathers, a queen sat sewing at the window, with an ebony frame. And as she was sewing and looking out at the snowflakes, she pricked her finger with her needle and three drops of blood fell on the snow. The red looked so beautiful on the white snow that she thought to herself: "If only I had a child as white as snow and as red as blood and as black as the wood of my window frame." A little while later she gave birth to a daughter, who was as white as snow and as red as blood, and her hair was as black as ebony. They called her Snow White, and when she was born, the queen died.

A year later the king took a second wife. She was beautiful, but she was proud and overbearing, and she couldn't bear the thought that anyone might be more beautiful than she. She had a magic mirror, and when she went up to it and looked at herself, she said:

---

1 First published in 1812/15, in the first edition of *Kinder- und Hausmärchen*. This text from the second edition (1819), from *Grimms' Tales for Young and Old*, trans. Ralph Manheim (Garden City, NY: Anchor P, 1977).

"Mirror, Mirror, here I stand.
 Who is the fairest in the land?"

and the mirror answered:

"You, O Queen, are the fairest in the land."

That set her mind at rest, for she knew the mirror told the truth.

But as Snow White grew, she became more and more beautiful, and by the time she was seven years old she was as beautiful as the day and more beautiful than the queen herself. One day when the queen said to her mirror:

"Mirror, Mirror, here I stand.
 Who is the fairest in the land?"

the mirror replied:

"You, O Queen, are the fairest here,
 But Snow White is a thousand times more fair."

The Queen gasped, and turned yellow and green with envy. Every time she laid eyes on Snow White after that she hated her so much that her heart turned over in her bosom. Envy and pride grew like weeds in her heart, until she knew no peace by day or by night. Finally she sent for a huntsman and said: "Get that child out of my sight. Take her into the forest and kill her and bring me her lungs and her liver to prove you've done it." The huntsman obeyed. He took the child out into the forest, but when he drew his hunting knife and prepared to pierce Snow White's innocent heart, she began to cry and said: "Oh, dear huntsman, let me live. I'll run off through the wild woods and never come home again." Because of her beauty the huntsman took pity on her and said: "All right, you poor child. Run away." To himself, he thought: "The wild beasts will soon eat her," but not having to kill her was a great weight off his mind all the same. Just then a young boar came bounding out of the thicket. The huntsman thrust his knife into it, took the lungs and liver and brought them to the queen as proof that he had done her bidding. The cook was ordered to salt and stew them, and the godless woman ate them, thinking she was eating Snow White's lungs and liver.

Meanwhile the poor child was all alone in the great forest. She was so afraid that she looked at all the leaves on the trees and didn't know what to do. She began to run, she ran over sharp stones and through brambles, and the wild beasts passed by without harming her. She ran as long as her legs would carry her and then, just before nightfall, she saw a little house and went in to rest. Inside the house everything was tiny, but wonderfully neat and clean. There was a table spread with a white cloth, and on the table there were seven little plates, each with its own knife, fork, and spoon, and seven little cups. Over against the wall there were seven little beds all in a row, covered with spotless white sheets. Snow White was very hungry and thirsty, but she didn't want to eat up anyone's entire meal, so she ate a bit of bread and vegetables from each plate and drank a sip of wine from each cup. Then she was so tired that she lay down on one of the beds, but none of the beds quite suited her; some were too long and some were too short, but the seventh was just right. There she stayed and when she had said her prayers she fell asleep.

When it was quite dark, the owners of the little house came home. They were seven dwarfs who went off to the mountains every day with their picks and shovels, to mine silver. They lit their seven little candles, and when the light went up they saw someone had been there, because certain things had been moved. The first said: "Who has been sitting in my chair?" The second: "Who has been eating off my plate?" The third: "Who has taken a bite of my bread?" The fourth: "Who has been eating some of my vegetables?" The fifth: "Who has been using my fork?" The sixth: "Who has been cutting with my knife?" And the seventh: "Who has been drinking out of my cup?" Then the first looked around, saw a little hollow in his bed and said: "Who has been lying in my bed?" The others came running, and cried out: "Somebody has been lying in my bed too." But when the seventh looked at his bed, he saw Snow White lying there asleep. He called the others, who came running. They cried out in amazement, went to get their seven little candles, and held them over Snow White: "Heavens above!" they cried. "Heavens above! What a beautiful child!" They were so delighted they didn't wake her but let her go on sleeping in the little bed. The seventh dwarf slept with his comrades, an hour with each one, and then the night was over.

Next morning Snow White woke up, and when she saw the seven dwarfs she was frightened. But they were friendly and asked: "What's your name?" "My name is Snow White," she said. "How did you get to our house?" the dwarfs asked. And she told them how her stepmother had wanted to kill her, how the huntsman had spared her life, and how she had walked all day until at last she found their little house. The dwarfs said: "If you will keep house for us, and do the cooking and make the beds and wash and sew and knit, and keep everything neat and clean, you can stay with us and you'll want for nothing." "Oh, yes," said Snow White. "I'd love to." So she stayed and kept the house in order, and in the morning they went off to the mountains to look for silver and gold, and in the evening they came home again and dinner had to be ready. But all day Snow White was alone, and the kindly dwarfs warned her, saying: "Watch out for your stepmother. She'll soon find out you're here. Don't let anyone in."

After eating Snow White's lungs and liver, the queen felt sure she was again the most beautiful of all. She went to her mirror and said:

"Mirror, Mirror, here I stand.
 Who is the fairest in the land?"

And the mirror replied:

"You, O Queen, are the fairest here,
 But Snow White, who has gone to stay
 With the seven dwarfs far, far away,
 Is a thousand times more fair."

The queen gasped. She knew the mirror told no lies and she realized that the huntsman had deceived her and that Snow White was still alive. She racked her brains for a way to kill her, because she simply had to be the fairest in the land, or envy would leave her no peace. At last she thought up a plan. She stained her face and dressed like an old peddler woman, so that no one could have recognized her. In this disguise she made her way across the seven mountains to the house of the seven dwarfs, knocked at the door and cried out: "Pretty things for sale! For sale!" Snow White looked out of the window and said: "Good day, old woman, what have you got to sell?" "Nice things, nice things!" she replied. "Laces, all colors," and she took out a lace woven of bright-colored silk. "This woman looks so honest," thought Snow White. "It must be all right to let her in." So she unbolted the door and bought the pretty lace. "Child!" said the old woman, "you look a fright. Come, let me lace you up properly." Suspecting nothing, Snow White stepped up and let the old woman put in the new lace. But she did it so quickly and pulled the lace so tight that Snow White's breath was cut off and she fell down as though dead. "Well, well," said the queen, "you're not the fairest in the land now." And she hurried away.

A little while later, at nightfall, the seven dwarfs came home. How horrified they were to see their beloved Snow White lying on the floor! She lay so still they thought she was dead. They lifted her up, and when they saw she was laced too tightly, they cut the lace. She breathed just a little, and then little by little she came to life. When the dwarfs heard what had happened, they said: "That old peddler woman was the wicked queen and no one else. You've got to be careful and never let anyone in when we're away."

When the wicked woman got home, she went to her mirror and asked:

"Mirror, Mirror, here I stand.

Who is the fairest in the land?"

And the mirror answered as usual:

> "You, O Queen, are the fairest here,
> But Snow White, who has gone to stay
> With the seven dwarfs far, far away,
> Is a thousand times more fair."

When she heard that, it gave her such a pang that the blood rushed to her heart, for she realized that Snow White had revived. "Never mind," she said. "I'll think up something now that will really destroy you," and with the help of some magic spells she knew she made a poisoned comb. Then she disguised herself and took the form of another old woman. And again she made her way over the seven mountains to the house of the seven dwarfs, knocked at the door and said: "Pretty things for sale! For sale!" Snow White looked out and said: "Go away. I can't let anyone in." "You can look, can't you?" said the old woman, taking out the poisoned comb and holding it up. The child liked it so well that she forgot everything else and opened the door. When they had agreed on the price, the old woman said: "Now I'll give your hair a proper combing." Suspecting nothing, poor Snow White stood still for the old woman, but no sooner had the comb touched her hair than the poison took effect and she fell into a dead faint. "There, my beauty," said the wicked woman. "It's all up with you now." And she went away. But luckily it wasn't long till nightfall. When the seven dwarfs came home and found Snow White lying on the floor as though dead, they immediately suspected the stepmother. They examined Snow White and found the poisoned comb, and no sooner had they pulled it out than she woke up and told them what had happened. Again they warned her to be on her guard and not to open the door to anyone.

When the queen got home she went to her mirror and said,

> "Mirror, Mirror, here I stand.
> Who is the fairest in the land?"

And the mirror answered as before:

> "You, O Queen, are the fairest here,
> But Snow White, who has gone to stay
> With the seven dwarfs far, far away,
> Is a thousand times more fair."

When she heard the mirror say that, she trembled and shook with rage. "Snow White must die!" she cried out. "Even if it costs me my own life." Then she went to a secret room that no one else knew about and made a very poisonous apple. It looked so nice on the outside, white with red cheeks, that anyone who saw it would want it; but anyone who ate even the tiniest bit of it would die. When the apple was ready, she stained her face and disguised herself as a peasant woman. And again she made her way across the seven mountains to the house of the seven dwarfs. She knocked at the door and Snow White put her head out of the window. "I can't let anyone in," she said. "The seven dwarfs won't let me." "It doesn't matter," said the peasant woman. "I only want to get rid of these apples. Here, I'll make you a present of one." "No," said Snow White. "I'm not allowed to take anything." "Are you afraid of poison?" said the old woman. "Look, I'm cutting it in half. You eat the red cheek and I'll eat the white cheek." But the apple had been so cleverly made that only the red cheek was poisoned. Snow White longed for the lovely apple, and when she saw the peasant woman taking a bite out of it she couldn't resist. She held out her hand and took the poisonous half. And no sooner had she taken a bite than she fell to the floor dead. The queen gave her a cruel look, laughed a terrible laugh, and said: "White as snow, red as blood, black as ebony. The dwarfs won't revive you this time." And when she got home and questioned the mirror:

"Mirror, Mirror, here I stand.
Who is the fairest in the land?"

The mirror answered at last:

"You, O Queen, are the fairest in the land."

Then her envious heart was at peace, insofar as an envious heart can be at peace.

When the dwarfs came home at nightfall, they found Snow White lying on the floor. No breath came out of her mouth and she was really dead. They lifted her up, looked to see if they could find anything poisonous, unlaced her, combed her hair, washed her in water and wine, but nothing helped; the dear child was dead, and dead she remained. They laid her on a bier, and all seven sat down beside it and mourned, and they wept for three whole days. Then they were going to bury her, but she still looked fresh and alive, and she still had her beautiful red cheeks. "We can't lower her into the black earth," they said, and they had a coffin made out of glass, so that she could be seen from all sides, and they put her into it and wrote her name in gold letters on the coffin, adding that she was a king's daughter. Then they put the coffin on the hilltop, and one of them always stayed there to guard it.

And the birds came and wept for Snow White, first an owl, then a raven, and then a dove.

Snow White lay in her coffin for years and years. She didn't rot, but continued to look as if she were asleep, for she was still as white as snow, as red as blood, and as black as ebony. Then one day a prince came to that forest and stopped for the night at the dwarfs' house. He saw the coffin on the hilltop, he saw lovely Snow White inside it, and he read the gold letters on the coffin. He said to the dwarfs: "Let me have the coffin, I'll pay you as much as you like for it." But the dwarfs replied: "We wouldn't part with it for all the money in the world." "Then give it to me," he said, "for I can't go on living unless I look at Snow White. I will honor and cherish her forever." Then the dwarfs took pity on him and gave him the coffin. The prince's servants hoisted it up on their shoulders and as they were carrying it away they stumbled over a root. The jolt shook the poisoned core, which Snow White had bitten off, out of her throat, and soon she opened her eyes, lifted the coffin lid, sat up, and was alive again. "Oh!" she cried. "Where am I?" "With me!" the prince answered joyfully. Then he told her what had happened and said: "I love you more than anything in the world; come with me to my father's castle and be my wife." Snow White loved him and went with him, and arrangements were made for a splendid wedding feast.

Snow White's wicked stepmother was among those invited to the wedding. When she had put on her fine clothes, she went to her mirror and said:

"Mirror, Mirror, here I stand.
Who is the fairest in the land?"

And the mirror answered:

"You, O Queen, are the fairest here.
But the young queen is a thousand times more fair."

At that the wicked woman spat out a curse. She was so horror-stricken she didn't know what to do. At first she didn't want to go to the wedding, but then she couldn't resist; she just had to go and see the young queen. The moment she entered the hall she recognized Snow White, and she was so terrified that she just stood there and couldn't move. But two iron slippers had already been put into glowing coals. Someone took them out with a pair of tongs and set them down in front of her. She was forced to step into the red-hot shoes and dance till she fell to the floor dead.

RAPUNZEL[1]

Jacob and Wilhelm Grimm

ONCE AFTER A MAN AND wife had long wished in vain for a child, the wife had reason to hope that God would grant them their wish. In the back of their house there was a little window that looked out over a wonderful garden, full of beautiful flowers and vegetables. But there was a high wall around the garden, and no one dared enter it because it belonged to a witch, who was very powerful and everyone was afraid of her. One day the wife stood at this window, looking down into the garden, and her eyes lit on a bed of the finest rapunzel, which is a kind of lettuce. And it looked so fresh and green that she longed for it and her mouth watered. Her craving for it grew from day to day, and she began to waste away because she knew she would never get any. Seeing her so pale and wretched, her husband took fright and asked: "What's the matter with you, dear wife?" "Oh," she said, "I shall die unless I get some rapunzel to eat from the garden behind our house." Her husband, who loved her, thought: "Sooner than let my wife die, I shall get her some of that rapunzel, cost what it may." As night was falling, he climbed the wall into the witch's garden, took a handful of rapunzel, and brought it to his wife. She made it into a salad right away and ate it hungrily. But it tasted so good, so very good, that the next day her craving for it was three times as great. Her husband could see she would know no peace unless he paid another visit to the garden. So at nightfall he climbed the wall again, but when he came down on the other side he had an awful fright, for there was the witch right in front of him. "How dare you!" she said with an angry look. "How dare you sneak into my garden like a thief and steal my rapunzel! I'll make you pay dearly for this." "Oh, please," he said, "please temper justice with mercy. I only did it because I had to. My wife was looking out of the window, and when she saw your rapunzel she felt such a craving for it that she would have died if I hadn't got her some." At that the witch's anger died down and she said: "If that's how it is, you may take as much rapunzel as you wish, but on one condition: that you give me the child your wife will bear. It will have a good life and I shall care for it like a mother." In his fright, the man agreed to everything, and the moment his wife was delivered, the witch appeared, gave the child the name of Rapunzel, and took her away.

Rapunzel grew to be the loveliest child under the sun. When she was twelve years old, the witch took her to the middle of the forest and shut her up in a tower that

---

1   First published in 1812/15, in the first edition of *Kinder- und Hausmärchen*. This text from the second edition
    (1819), from *Grimms' Tales for Young and Old*, trans. Ralph Manheim (Garden City, NY: Anchor P, 1977).

had neither stairs nor door, but only a little window at the very top. When the witch wanted to come in, she stood down below and called out: "Rapunzel, Rapunzel, Let down your hair for me." Rapunzel had beautiful long hair, as fine as spun gold. When she heard the witch's voice, she undid her braids and fastened them to the window latch. They fell to the ground twenty ells down, and the witch climbed up on them.

A few years later it so happened that the king's son was passing through the forest. When he came to the tower, he heard someone singing, and the singing was so lovely that he stopped and listened. It was Rapunzel, who in her loneliness was singing to pass the time. The prince wanted to go up to her and he looked for a door but found none. He rode away home, but the singing had so touched his heart that he went out into the forest every day and listened. Once as he was standing behind a tree, he saw a witch come to the foot of the tower and heard her call out:

"Rapunzel, Rapunzel,
Let down your hair."

Whereupon Rapunzel let down her braids, and the witch climbed up to her. "Aha," he thought, "if that's the ladder that goes up to her, then I'll try my luck too." And next day, when it was beginning to get dark, he went to the tower and called out:

"Rapunzel, Rapunzel,
Let down your hair."

A moment later her hair fell to the ground and the prince climbed up.

At first Rapunzel was dreadfully frightened, for she had never seen a man before, but the prince spoke gently to her and told her how he had been so moved by her singing that he couldn't rest easy until he had seen her. At that Rapunzel lost her fear, and when he asked if she would have him as her husband and she saw he was young and handsome, she thought: "He will love me better than my old godmother." So she said yes and put her hand in his hand. "I'd gladly go with you," she said, "but how will I ever get down? Every time you come, bring a skein of silk and I'll make a ladder with it. When it's finished, I'll climb down, and you will carry me home on your horse." They agreed that in the meantime he would come every evening, because the old witch came during the day. The witch noticed nothing until one day Rapunzel said to her: "Tell me, Godmother, how is it that you're so much harder to pull up than the young prince? With him it hardly takes a minute." "Wicked child!" cried the witch. "What did you say? I thought I had shut you away from the world, but you've deceived me." In her fury she seized Rapunzel's beautiful hair, wound it several times around her left hand and picked up a pair of scissors in her right hand. Snippety-snap went the scissors, and the lovely braids fell to the floor. Then the heartless witch sent poor Rapunzel to a desert place, where she lived in misery and want.

At dusk on the day she had sent Rapunzel away, she fastened the severed braids to the window latch, and when the prince came and called: "Rapunzel, Rapunzel, Let down your hair," she let the hair down. The prince climbed up, but instead of his dearest Rapunzel, the witch was waiting for him with angry, poisonous looks. "Aha!" she cried. "You've come to take your darling wife away, but the bird is gone from the nest, she won't be singing any more; the cat has taken her away and before she's done she'll scratch your eyes out too. You've lost Rapunzel, you'll never see her again." The prince was beside himself with grief, and in his despair he jumped from the tower. It didn't kill him, but the brambles he fell into scratched his eyes out and he was blind. He wandered through the forest, living on roots and berries and weeping and wailing over the loss of his dearest wife. For several years he wandered wretchedly, until at last he came to the desert place where Rapunzel was living in misery with the twins she had born—a boy and a girl. He heard a voice that seemed familiar, and when he approached Rapunzel recognized him, fell on his neck and wept. Two of her tears dropped on his eyes, which were made clear again, so that he could see as well as ever. He took her to his kingdom, where she was welcomed with rejoicing, and they lived happy and contented for many years to come.

JACK AND THE BEANSTALK[1]

Joseph Jacobs

THERE WAS ONCE UPON A time a poor widow who had an only son named Jack, and a cow named Milky-white. And all they had to live on was the milk the cow gave every morning, which they carried to the market and sold. But one morning Milky-white gave no milk, and they didn't know what to do.

"What shall we do, what shall we do?" said the widow, wringing her hands.

"Cheer up, mother, I'll go and get work somewhere," said Jack.

"We've tried that before, and nobody would take you," said his mother; "we must sell Milky-white and with the money start shop, or something."

"All right, mother," says Jack; "it's market-day today, and I'll soon sell Milky-white, and then we'll see what we can do."

---

1   From *English Fairy Tales*, 1890 (repr. New York: Dover, 1967).

So he took the cow's halter in his hand, and off he started. He hadn't gone far when he met a funny-looking old man, who said to him: "Good morning, Jack."

"Good morning to you," said Jack, and wondered how he knew his name.

"Well, Jack, and where are you off to?" said the man.

"I'm going to market to sell our cow here."

"Oh, you look the proper sort of chap to sell cows," said the man; "I wonder if you know how many beans make five."

"Two in each hand and one in your mouth," says Jack, as sharp as a needle.

"Right you are," says the man, "and here they are, the very beans themselves," he went on, pulling out of his pocket a number of strange-looking beans. "As you are so sharp," says he, "I don't mind doing a swap with you—your cow for these beans."

"Go along," says Jack; "wouldn't you like it?"

"Ah! you don't know what these beans are," said the man; "if you plant them over-night, by morning they grow right up to the sky."

"Really?" said Jack; "you don't say so."

"Yes, that is so, and if it doesn't turn out to be true you can have your cow back."

"Right," says Jack, and hands him over Milky-white's halter and pockets the beans.

Back goes Jack home, and as he hadn't gone very far it wasn't dusk by the time he got to his door.

"Back already, Jack?" said his mother; "I see you haven't got Milky-white, so you've sold her. How much did you get for her?"

"You'll never guess, mother," says Jack.

"No, you don't say so. Good boy! Five pounds, ten, fifteen, no, it can't be twenty."

"I told you you couldn't guess. What do you say to these beans; they're magical, plant them overnight and—"

"What!" says Jack's mother, "have you been such a fool, such a dolt, such an idiot, as to give away my Milky-white, the best milker in the parish, and prime beef to boot, for a set of paltry beans? Take that! Take that! Take that! And as for your precious beans here they go out of the window. And now off with you to bed. Not a sup shall you drink, and not a bit shall you swallow this very night."

So Jack went upstairs to his little room in the attic, and sad and sorry he was, to be sure, as much for his mother's sake, as for the loss of his supper.

At last he dropped off to sleep.

When he woke up, the room looked so funny. The sun was shining into part of it, and yet all the rest was quite dark and shady. So Jack jumped up and dressed himself and went to the window. And what do you think he saw? Why, the beans his mother had thrown out of the window into the garden had sprung up into a big beanstalk which went up and up and up till it reached the sky. So the man spoke truth after all.

The beanstalk grew up quite close past Jack's window, so all he had to do was to open it and give a jump on to the beanstalk which ran up just like a big ladder. So Jack climbed, and he climbed and he climbed and he climbed and he climbed and he climbed and he climbed till at last he reached the sky. And when he got there he found a long broad road going as straight as a dart. So he walked along and he walked along and he walked along till he came to a great big tall house, and on the doorstep there was a great big tall woman.

"Good morning, mum," says Jack, quite polite-like. "Could you be so kind as to give me some breakfast?" For he hadn't had anything to eat, you know, the night before and was as hungry as a hunter.

"It's breakfast you want, is it?" says the great big tall woman, "It's breakfast you'll be if you don't move off from here. My man is an ogre and there's nothing he likes better than boys broiled on toast. You'd better be moving on or he'll soon be coming."

"Oh! please mum, do give me something to eat, mum. I've had nothing to eat since yesterday morning, really and truly, mum," says Jack. "I may as well be broiled as die of hunger."

Well, the ogre's wife was not half so bad after all. So she took Jack into the kitchen, and gave him a hunk of bread and cheese and a jug of milk. But Jack hadn't half finished these when thump! thump! thump! the whole house began to tremble with the noise of some one coming.

"Goodness gracious me! It's my old man," said the ogre's wife, "what on earth shall I do? Come along quick and jump in here." And she bundled Jack into the oven just as the ogre came in.

He was a big one, to be sure. At his belt he had three calves strung up by the heels, and he unhooked them and threw them down on the table and said: "Here, wife, broil me a couple of these for breakfast. Ah! what's this I smell?

Fee-fi-fo-fum,
I smell the blood of an Englishman,
Be he alive, or be he dead
I'll have his bones to grind my bread."

"Nonsense dear," said his wife, "you're dreaming. Or perhaps you smell the scraps of that little boy you liked so much for yesterday's dinner. Here, you go and have a wash and tidy up, and by the time you come back your breakfast'll be ready for you."

So off the ogre went, and Jack was just going to jump out of the oven and run away when the woman told him not. "Wait till he's asleep," says she; "he always has a doze after breakfast."

Well, the ogre had his breakfast, and after that he goes to a big chest and takes out of it a couple of bags of gold, and down he sits and counts till at last his head began to nod and he began to snore till the whole house shook again.

Then Jack crept out on tiptoe from his oven, and as he was passing the ogre he took one of the bags of gold under his arm, and off he pelters till he came to the beanstalk, and then he threw down the bag of gold, which of course fell into his mother's garden, and then he climbed down and climbed down till at last he got home and told his mother and showed her the gold and said: "Well, mother, wasn't I right about the beans? They are really magical, you see."

So they lived on the bag of gold for some time, but at last they came to the end of it, and Jack made up his mind to try his luck once more up at the top of the beanstalk. So one fine morning he rose up early, and got on to the beanstalk, and he climbed and he climbed and he climbed and he climbed and he climbed and he climbed till at last he came out on to the road again and up to the great big tall house he had been to before. There, sure enough, was the great big tall woman standing on the doorstep.

"Good morning, mum," says Jack, as bold as brass, "could you be so good as to give me something to eat?"

"Go away, my boy," said the big tall woman, "or else my man will eat you for breakfast. But aren't you the youngster who came here once before? Do you know, that very day, my man missed one of his bags of gold."

"That's strange, mum," said Jack, "I dare say I could tell you something about that, but I'm so hungry I can't speak till I've had something to eat."

Well the big tall woman was so curious that she took him in and gave him something to eat. But he had scarcely begun munching it as slowly as he could when thump! thump! thump! they heard the giant's footstep, and his wife hid Jack away in the oven.

All happened as it did before. In came the ogre as he did before, said: "Fee-fi-fo-fum," and had his breakfast of three broiled oxen. Then he said: "Wife, bring me the hen that lays the golden eggs." So she brought it, and the ogre said: "Lay," and it laid an egg all of gold. And then the ogre began to nod his head, and to snore till the house shook.

Then Jack crept out of the oven on tiptoe and caught hold of the golden hen, and was off before you could say "Jack Robinson." But this time the hen gave a cackle which woke the ogre, and just as Jack got out of the house he heard him calling: "Wife, wife, what have you done with my golden hen?"

And the wife said: "Why, my dear?"

But that was all Jack heard, for he rushed off to the beanstalk and climbed down like a house on fire. And when he got home he showed his mother the wonderful hen, and said "Lay" to it; and it laid a golden egg every time he said "Lay."

Well, Jack was not content, and it wasn't very long before he determined to have another try at his luck up there at the top of the beanstalk. So one fine morning, he rose up early, and got on to the beanstalk, and he climbed and he climbed and he climbed and he climbed till he got to the top. But this time he knew better than to go straight to the ogre's house. And when he got near it, he waited behind a bush till he saw the ogre's wife come out with a pail to get some water, and then he crept into the house and got into the copper.[1] He hadn't been there long when he heard thump! thump! thump! as before, and in come the ogre and his wife.

"Fee-fi-fo-fum, I smell the blood of an Englishman," cried out the ogre. "I smell him, wife, I smell him."

"Do you, my dearie?" says the ogre's wife. "Then, if it's that little rogue that stole your gold and the hen that laid the golden eggs he's sure to have got into the oven." And they both rushed to the oven. But Jack wasn't there, luckily, and the ogre's wife said: "There you are again with your fee-fi-fo-fum. Why of course it's the boy you caught last night that I've just broiled for your breakfast. How forgetful I am, and how careless you are not to know the difference between live and dead after all these years."

So the ogre sat down to the breakfast and ate it, but every now and then he would mutter: "Well, I could have sworn—" and he'd get up and search the larder and the cupboards and everything, only, luckily, he didn't think of the copper.

After breakfast was over, the ogre called out: "Wife, wife, bring me my golden harp." So she brought it and put it on the table before him. Then he said: "Sing!" and the golden harp sang most beautifully. And it went on singing till the ogre fell asleep, and commenced to snore like thunder.

Then Jack lifted up the copper-lid very quietly and got down like a mouse and crept on hands and knees till he came to the table, when up he crawled, caught hold of the golden harp and dashed with it towards the door. But the harp called out quite loud: "Master! Master!" and the ogre woke up just in time to see Jack running off with his harp.

Jack ran as fast as he could, and the ogre came rushing after, and would soon have caught him only Jack had a start and dodged him a bit and knew where he was going. When he got to the beanstalk the ogre was not more than twenty yards away when suddenly he saw Jack disappear like, and when he came to the end of the road he saw Jack underneath climbing down for dear life. Well, the ogre didn't like trusting himself to such a ladder, and he stood and waited, so Jack got another start. But just then the harp cried out: "Master! Master!" and the ogre swung himself down on to the beanstalk, which shook with his weight. Down climbs Jack, and after him climbed the ogre. By this time Jack had climbed down and climbed down and climbed down till he was very nearly home. So he called out: "Mother! Mother! bring me an axe, bring me an axe." And his mother came rushing out with the axe in her hand, but

---

1   Copper: A large metal pot for boiling laundry.

when she came to the beanstalk she stood stock still with fright for there she saw the ogre with his legs just through the clouds.

But Jack jumped down and got hold of the axe and gave a chop at the beanstalk which cut it half in two. The ogre felt the beanstalk shake and quiver so he stopped to see what was the matter. Then Jack gave another chop with the axe, and the beanstalk was cut in two and began to topple over. Then the ogre fell down and broke his crown, and the beanstalk came toppling after.

Then Jack showed his mother his golden harp, and what with showing that and selling the golden eggs, Jack and his mother became very rich, and he married a great princess, and they lived happy ever after.

THE UGLY DUCKLING[1]

Hans Christian Andersen

IT WAS SO BEAUTIFUL OUT in the country. It was summer. The oats were still green, but the wheat was turning yellow. Down in the meadow the grass had been cut and made into haystacks; and there the storks walked on their long red legs talking Egyptian, because that was the language they had been taught by their mothers. The fields were enclosed by woods, and hidden among them were little lakes and pools. Yes, it certainly was lovely out there in the country!

The old castle, with its deep moat surrounding it, lay bathed in sunshine. Between the heavy walls and the edge of the moat there was a narrow strip of land covered by a whole forest of burdock plants. Their leaves were large and some of the stalks were so tall that a child could stand upright under them and imagine that he was in the middle of the wild and lonely woods. Here a duck had built her nest. While she sat waiting for the eggs to hatch, she felt a little sorry for herself because it was taking so long and hardly anybody came to visit her. The other ducks preferred swimming in the moat to sitting under a dock leaf and gossiping.

Finally the eggs began to crack. "Peep … Peep," they said one after another. The egg yolks had become alive and were sticking out their heads.

"Quack … Quack …" said their mother. "Look around you." And the ducklings did; they glanced at the green world about them, and that was what their mother wanted them to do, for green was good for their eyes.

---

1 First published in 1843. This text from *Hans Christian Andersen: His Classic Fairy Tales,* trans. Erik Haugaard (New York: Doubleday, 1974).

"How big the world is!" piped the little ones, for they had much more space to move around in now than they had had inside the egg.

"Do you think that this is the whole world?" quacked their mother. "The world is much larger than this. It stretches as far as the minister's wheat fields, though I have not been there…. Are you all here?" The duck got up and turned around to look at her nest. "Oh no, the biggest egg hasn't hatched yet; and I'm so tired of sitting here! I wonder how long it will take?" she wailed, and sat down again.

"What's new?" asked an old duck who had come visiting.

"One of the eggs is taking so long," complained the mother duck. "It won't crack. But take a look at the others. They are the sweetest little ducklings you have ever seen; and every one of them looks exactly like their father. That scoundrel hasn't come to visit me once."

"Let me look at the egg that won't hatch," demanded the old duck. "I am sure that it's a turkey egg! I was fooled that way once. You can't imagine what it's like. Turkeys are afraid of the water. I couldn't get them to go into it. I quacked and I nipped them, but nothing helped. Let me see that egg! … Yes, it's a turkey egg. Just let it lie there. You go and teach your young ones how to swim, that's my advice."

"I have sat on it so long that I suppose I can sit a little longer, at least until they get the hay in," replied the mother duck.

"Suit yourself," said the older duck, and went on.

At last the big egg cracked too. "Peep … Peep," said the young one, and tumbled out. He was big and very ugly.

The mother duck looked at him. "He's awfully big for his age," she said. "He doesn't look like any of the others. I wonder if he could be a turkey? Well, we shall soon see. Into the water he will go, even if I have to kick him to make him do it."

The next day the weather was gloriously beautiful. The sun shone on the forest of burdock plants. The mother duck took her whole brood to the moat. "Quack … Quack …" she ordered.

One after another, the little ducklings plunged into the water. For a moment their heads disappeared, but then they popped up again and the little ones floated like so many corks. Their legs knew what to do without being told. All of the new brood swam very nicely, even the ugly one.

"He is no turkey," mumbled the mother. "See how beautifully he uses his legs and how straight he holds his neck. He is my own child and, when you look closely at him, he's quite handsome…. Quack! Quack! Follow me and I'll take you to the henyard and introduce you to everyone. But stay close to me, so that no one steps on you, and look out for the cat."

They heard an awful noise when they arrived at the henyard. Two families of ducks had got into a fight over the head of an eel. Neither of them got it, for it was swiped by the cat.

"That is the way of the world," said the mother duck, and licked her bill. She would have liked to have had the eel's head herself. "Walk nicely," she admonished them. "And remember to bow to the old duck over there. She has Spanish blood in her veins and is the most aristocratic fowl here. That is why she is so fat and has a red rag tied around one of her legs. That is the highest mark of distinction a duck can be given. It means so much that she will never be done away with; and all the other fowl and the human beings know who she is. Quack! Quack!… Don't walk, waddle like well-brought-up ducklings. Keep your legs far apart, just as your mother and father have always done. Bow your heads and say, 'Quack'!" And that was what the little ducklings did.

Other ducks gathered about them and said loudly, "What do we want that gang here for? Aren't there enough of us already? Pooh! Look how ugly one of them is! He's the last straw!" And one of the ducks flew over and bit the ugly duckling on the neck.

"Leave him alone!" shouted the mother. "He hasn't done anyone any harm."

"He's big and he doesn't look like everybody else!" replied the duck who had bitten him. "And that's reason enough to beat him."

"Very good-looking children you have," remarked the duck with the red rag around one of her legs. "All of them are beautiful except one. He didn't turn out very well. I wish you could make him over again."

"That's not possible, Your Grace," answered the mother duck. "He may not be handsome, but he has a good character and swims as well as the others, if not a little better. Perhaps he will grow handsomer as he grows older and becomes a bit smaller. He was in the egg too long, and that is why he doesn't have the right shape." She smoothed his neck for a moment and then added, "Besides, he's a drake; and it doesn't matter so much what he looks like. He is strong and I am sure he will be able to take care of himself."

"Well, the others are nice," said the old duck. "Make yourself at home, and if you should find an eel's head, you may bring it to me."

And they were "at home."

The poor little duckling, who had been the last to hatch and was so ugly, was bitten and pushed and made fun of both by the hens and by the other ducks. The turkey cock (who had been born with spurs on, and therefore thought he was an emperor) rustled his feathers as if he were a full-rigged ship under sail, and strutted up to the duckling. He gobbled so loudly at him that his own face got all red.

The poor little duckling did not know where to turn. How he grieved over his own ugliness, and how sad he was! The poor creature was mocked and laughed at by the whole henyard.

That was the first day; and each day that followed was worse than the one before. The poor duckling was chased and mistreated by everyone, even his own sisters and brothers, who quacked again and again, "If only the cat would get you, you ugly thing!"

Even his mother said, "I wish you were far away." The other ducks bit him and the hens pecked at him. The little girl who came to feed the fowls kicked him.

At last the duckling ran away. He flew over the tops of the bushes, frightening all the little birds so that they flew up into the air. "They, too, think I am ugly," thought the duckling, and closed his eyes—but he kept on running.

Finally he came to a great swamp where wild ducks lived; and here he stayed for the night, for he was too tired to go any farther.

In the morning he was discovered by the wild ducks. They looked at him and one of them asked, "What kind of bird are you?"

The ugly duckling bowed in all directions, for he was trying to be as polite as he knew how.

"You are ugly," said the wild ducks, "but that is no concern of ours, as long as you don't try to marry into our family."

The poor duckling wasn't thinking of marriage. All he wanted was to be allowed to swim among the reeds and drink a little water when he was thirsty.

He spent two days in the swamp; then two wild geese came—or rather, two wild ganders, for they were males. They had been hatched not long ago; therefore they were both frank and bold.

"Listen, comrade," they said. "You are so ugly that we like you. Do you want to migrate with us? Not far from here there is a marsh where some beautiful wild geese live. They are all lovely maidens, and you are so ugly that you may seek your fortune among them. Come along."

"Bang! Bang!" Two shots were heard and both ganders fell down dead among the reeds, and the water turned red from their blood.

"Bang! Bang!" Again came the sound of shots, and a flock of wild geese flew up.

The whole swamp was surrounded by hunters; from every direction came the awful noise. Some of the hunters had hidden behind bushes or among the reeds but others, screened from sight by the leaves, sat on the long, low branches of the trees that stretched out over the swamp. The blue smoke from the guns lay like a fog over the water and along the trees. Dogs came splashing through the marsh, and they bent and broke the reeds.

The poor little duckling was terrified. He was about to tuck his head under his wing, in order to hide, when he saw a big dog peering at him through the reeds. The dog's tongue hung out of its mouth and its eyes glistened evilly. It bared its teeth. Splash! It turned away without touching the duckling.

"Oh, thank God!" he sighed. "I am so ugly that even the dog doesn't want to bite me."

The little duckling lay as still as he could while the shots whistled through the reeds. Not until the middle of the afternoon did the shooting stop; but the poor little duckling was still so frightened that he waited several hours longer before taking his head out from under his wing. Then he ran as quickly as he could out of the swamp. Across the fields and the meadows he went, but a wind had come up and he found it hard to make his way against it.

Towards evening he came upon a poor little hut. It was so wretchedly crooked that it looked as if it couldn't make up its mind which way to fall and that was why it was still standing. The wind was blowing so hard that the poor little duckling had to sit down in order not to be blown away. Suddenly he noticed that the door was off its hinges, making a crack; and he squeezed himself through it and was inside.

An old woman lived in the hut with her cat and her hen. The cat was called Sonny and could both arch his back and purr. Oh yes, it could also make sparks if you rubbed its fur the wrong way. The hen had very short legs and that was why she was called Cluck Lowlegs. But she was good at laying eggs, and the old woman loved her as if she were her own child.

In the morning the hen and the cat discovered the duckling. The cat meowed and the hen clucked.

"What is going on?" asked the old woman, and looked around. She couldn't see very well, and when she found the duckling she thought it was a fat, full-grown duck. "What a fine catch!" she exclaimed. "Now we shall have duck eggs, unless it's a drake. We'll give it a try."

So the duckling was allowed to stay for three weeks on probation, but he laid no eggs. The cat was the master of the house and the hen the mistress. They always referred to themselves as "we and the world," for they thought that they were half the world—and the better half at that. The duckling thought that he should be allowed to have a different opinion, but the hen did not agree.

"Can you lay eggs?" she demanded.

"No," answered the duckling.

"Then keep your mouth shut."

And the cat asked, "Can you arch your back? Can you purr? Can you make sparks?"

"No."

"Well, in that case, you have no right to have an opinion when sensible people are talking."

The duckling was sitting in a corner and was in a bad mood. Suddenly he recalled how lovely it could be outside in the fresh air when the sun shone: a great longing to be floating in the water came over the duckling, and he could not help talking about it.

"What is the matter with you?" asked the hen as soon as she had heard what he had to say. "You have nothing to do, that's why you get ideas like that. Lay eggs or purr, and such notions will disappear."

"You have no idea how delightful it is to float in the water, and to dive down to the bottom of a lake and get your head wet," said the duckling.

"Yes, that certainly does sound amusing," said the hen. "You must have gone mad. Ask the cat—he is the most intelligent being I know—ask him whether he likes to swim or dive down to the bottom of a lake. Don't take my word for anything…. Ask the old woman, who is the cleverest person in the world; ask her whether she likes to float and to get her head all wet."

"You don't understand me!" wailed the duckling.

"And if I don't understand you, who will? I hope you don't think that you are wiser than the cat or the old woman—not to mention myself. Don't give yourself airs! Thank your Creator for all He has done for you. Aren't you sitting in a warm room, where you can hear intelligent conversation that you could learn something from? While you, yourself, do nothing but say a lot of nonsense and aren't the least bit amusing! Believe me, that's the truth, and I am only telling it to you for your own good. That's how you recognize a true friend: it's someone who is willing to tell you the truth, no matter how unpleasant it is. Now get to work: lay some eggs, or learn to purr and arch your back."

"I think I'll go out into the wide world," replied the duckling.

"Go right ahead!" said the hen.

And the duckling left. He found a lake where he could float in the water and dive to the bottom. There were other ducks, but they ignored him because he was so ugly.

Autumn came and the leaves turned yellow and brown, then they fell from the trees. The wind caught them and made them dance. The clouds were heavy with hail and snow. A raven sat on a fence and screeched, "Ach! Ach!" because it was so cold. When just thinking of how cold it was is enough to make one shiver, what a terrible time the duckling must have had.

One evening just as the sun was setting gloriously, a flock of beautiful birds came out from among the rushes. Their feathers were so white that they glistened; and they had long, graceful necks. They were swans. They made a very loud cry, then they spread their powerful wings. They were flying south to a warmer climate, where the lakes were not frozen in the winter. Higher and higher they circled. The ugly duckling turned round and round in the water like a wheel and stretched his neck up toward the sky; he felt a strange longing. He screeched so piercingly that he frightened himself.

Oh, he would never forget those beautiful birds, those happy birds. When they were out of sight the duckling dived down under the water to the bottom of the lake; and when he came up again he was beside himself. He did not know the name of those birds or where they were going, and yet he felt he loved them as he had never loved any other creatures. He did not envy them. It did not even occur to him to wish that he were so handsome himself. He would have been happy if the other ducks had let him stay in the henyard: that poor, ugly bird!

The weather grew colder and colder. The duckling had to swim round and round in the water, to keep just a little space for himself that wasn't frozen. Each night his hole became smaller and smaller. On all sides of him the ice creaked and groaned. The little duckling had to keep his feet constantly in motion so that the last bit of open water wouldn't become ice. At last he was too tired to swim any more. He sat still. The ice closed in around him and he was frozen fast.

Early the next morning a farmer saw him and with his clogs broke the ice to free the duckling. The man put the bird under his arm and took it home to his wife, who brought the duckling back to life.

The children wanted to play with him. But the duckling was afraid that they were going to hurt him, so he flapped his wings and flew right into the milk pail. From there he flew into a big bowl of butter and then into a barrel of flour. What a sight he was!

The farmer's wife yelled and chased him with a poker. The children laughed and almost fell on top of each other, trying to catch him; and how they screamed! Luckily for the duckling, the door was open. He got out of the house and found a hiding place beneath some bushes, in the newly fallen snow; and there he lay so still, as though there was hardly any life left in him.

It would be too horrible to tell of all the hardship and suffering the duckling experienced that long winter. It is enough to know that he did survive. When again the sun shone warmly and the larks began to sing, the duckling was lying among the reeds in the swamp. Spring had come!

He spread out his wings to fly. How strong and powerful they were! Before he knew it, he was far from the swamp and flying above a beautiful garden. The apple trees were blooming and the lilac bushes stretched their flower-covered branches over the water of a winding canal. Everything was so beautiful: so fresh and green. Out of a forest of rushes came three swans. They ruffled their feathers and floated so lightly on the water. The ugly duckling recognized the birds and felt again that strange sadness come over him.

"I shall fly over to them, those royal birds! And they can hack me to death because I, who am so ugly, dare to approach them! What difference does it make? It is better to be killed by them than to be bitten by the other ducks, and pecked by the hens, and kicked by the girl who tends the henyard; or to suffer through the winter."

And he lighted on the water and swam towards the magnificent swans. When they saw him they ruffled their feathers and started to swim in his direction. They were coming to meet him.

"Kill me," whispered the poor creature, and bent his head humbly while he waited for death. But what was that he saw in the water? It was his own reflection; and he was no longer an awkward, clumsy, grey bird, so ungainly and so ugly. He was a swan!

It does not matter that one has been born in the henyard as long as one has lain in a swan's egg.

He was thankful that he had known so much want, and gone through so much suffering, for it made him appreciate his present happiness and the loveliness of everything about him all the more. The swans made a circle around him and caressed him with their beaks.

Some children came out into the garden. They had brought bread with them to feed the swans. The youngest child shouted, "Look, there's a new one!" All the children joyfully clapped their hands, and they ran to tell their parents.

Cake and bread were cast on the water for the swans. Everyone agreed that the new swan was the most beautiful of them all. The older swans bowed towards him.

He felt so shy that he hid his head beneath his wing. He was too happy, but not proud, for a kind heart can never be proud. He thought of the time when he had been mocked and persecuted. And now everyone said that he was the most beautiful of the most beautiful birds. And the lilac bushes stretched their branches right down to the water for him. The sun shone so warm and brightly. He ruffled his feathers and raised his slender neck, while out of the joy in his heart, he thought, "Such happiness I did not dream of when I was the ugly duckling."

ILLUSTRATION

NO PUBLISHER NOWADAYS WOULD DREAM of trying to sell a volume of fairy tales that was not accompanied by illustrations; indeed, one might be forgiven for thinking that the illustrator is sometimes of greater importance than the tales, which are chosen primarily as suitable vehicles for his or her artistic prowess. Indeed, the modern fairy-tale book consists, as often as not, of a single tale told primarily in pictures: the text has become a secondary consideration. It's an intriguing question, whether the inclusion of illustrations stifles the reader's imagination by imposing a visual representation upon it, or whether the pictures actually enhance the reader's imaginative response to the story. Clearly there are many factors involved, such as the age of the reader, the ability of the artist, and the meanings suggested by the illustrations. Yet even if we were able somehow to calculate relative values for such factors, how could we then compare the quality of the reader's response with and without the presence of illustrations? Calculations aside, there can be no question but that pictures add one more dimension to the various imaginative experiences of reading a tale, being read a tale, and being *told* a tale.

The origin of the fairy tale is oral, which accounts for its unique qualities: the emphasis upon action, the lack of physical detail, and the quick movement from one event to another—all ideally suited to the art of the storyteller. Furthermore, a tale can be told in many different ways, its impact upon the audience deriving from the intention, approach, and abilities of the teller. As we have seen, however, the evolution of the oral tale into printed text has all but obliterated the services of the storyteller, leaving room for the intercession of a new intermediary. Although without a teller there is no story, it can reasonably be argued that without an illustrator, the text is still there on the printed page, and yet, as Perry Nodelman points out in his instructive book *Words About Pictures*, our imaginations can rarely achieve the vividness and specificity that can be found in a good illustration. To achieve these qualities, both teller and illustrator must give something of themselves to the tale in order to infuse it with new life, since in its "basic" form, the tale leaves ample scope for the inventiveness of both contributors, as they work within the familiar framework of the story to create something new.

For example, one significant challenge for the artist is the depiction of characters familiar in name but not in image; he or she presumes thus to make explicit what is vague in the tales (we are told no more than that Little Red Riding Hood is "a pretty little girl," and the only thing we learn about Jack is that he "look[s] the proper sort of chap to sell cows"!). Alternatively, the artist may choose to concentrate upon the setting of the tale, giving a specificity to time and place that is denied by the traditional beginning of "once upon a time." Most important, however, is the interpretation of the events an illustration can provide. Indeed, the opportunity to expand and interpret has also been exploited by recorders of the tales, for as we noted earlier, Perrault and the Grimms were quite prepared to leave their mark on the tales, in the process of making them more suitable for their respective audiences. There is, of course, no guarantee that the embellishment provided by teller or artist will necessarily enrich the tale: we all know how painful an experience it can be to listen to a flat, indifferent reading of a tale, or how disappointed we feel when confronted by illustrations that do little more than fill space on the page. However, as Nodelman points out, illustrators, like the storytellers before them, have the power to transform the tale into a rich and meaningful tapestry.

We are told that every picture tells a story; an illustration tells at least two, for not only does it provide a visual dimension for the story it accompanies, but it also reveals something of the assumptions and values of the artist and of the culture to which he or she belongs. In this sense, illustrators are no different from the storytellers or the fairy-tale compilers of the past who inevitably kept an eye on their audience, making sure their material was both suitable and satisfying. As a result, the pictures that accompany fairy tales are often as much of a mirror as are the tales themselves.

Thus the encounter between the text and the reader's imagination is made more complex by the contribution of the illustrator, who imposes his or her particular vision and tone upon the narrative. Just how completely the reading of a tale can be influenced by different artists' interpretations will be demonstrated in the following pages: though the words may remain the same (or similar), the pictures tell us a different story. At the outset we commented that no modern publisher would seriously consider producing a book of fairy tales without illustrations; we might now add that few would publish such a book without illustrations in color. At the same time, the black-and-white originals that are included in our selection provide convincing evidence that the artist's decision not to use color does not signify a lesser commitment to the story. We have chosen examples of illustrative work that range from the last century to the present day. It is admittedly a very partial selection, since the number of illustrated versions of fairy tales has increased so dramatically in recent years. However, it may serve to give some indication of the variety of approaches that certain artists have adopted over the years—and hopefully to provide the student with some stimulus to seek out the work of others.

LITTLE RED RIDING HOOD

As we pointed out in our introduction to this tale, there is more to the story than a simple warning to children not to speak to strangers—and one artist whose work manifests abundant awareness of that fact is Gustave Doré (1832-83). The fact that Doré's work (published in 1863) is one of the earliest examples of fairy-tale illustration makes his insight into Perrault's tales all the more remarkable, not least because his engravings are of course without the benefit (or is it the distraction?) of color. Like many other artists since, he illustrates a critical moment in this story: the meeting between Little Red Riding Hood and the wolf (Figure 1). Absent, however, is the anthropomorphic interpretation of the wolf that many subsequent illustrators have adopted; this wolf is every inch a wolf. Nevertheless, Doré provides us with a carefully detailed portrait of the relationship between the two characters, which foreshadows the outcome of their encounter. As is often the case in Doré's work, the eyes are the focal point of the picture, in this instance, the fascinated gaze that binds prey to predator. Doré makes this a claustrophobic picture, as the little girl finds herself hemmed in by the wolf, whose proximity appears at first glance to be protective; its impact is all the more effective because the observer alone knows that deception and malice are at work here. Subtler still is the detail of the girl's unfastened shoe-strap, indicative of her vulnerability, her un-preparedness for harsh experience. As the little girl gazes up at the wolf as if hypnotized, her whole body expresses a naive trust and uncertainty. Although the wolf is depicted from a highly unusual perspective creating the effect of an upright human stance, Doré still manages to include his penetrating stare. That, together with the half-protective, half-suggestive movement of his hindquarters toward Little Red Riding Hood, reveals to the discerning eye what is to follow ...

Sarah Moon (b. 1941) focuses on the same fateful episode in her illustration (Figure 2, 1983), only this time in very different surroundings. Locating the tale in a modern but dated urban context and using the "truthful" medium of photography to illustrate the story momentarily frustrate the reader's expectations—but once the associative leap is made, the story's impact is irresistible, so striking and apposite

ILLUSTRATION

is Moon's imagery. Equally surprising is how similar Moon's treatment is to Doré's, over a hundred years earlier. The girl is a startled creature caught in the glare of the car's headlights, the darkness of the street creates the same claustrophobic effect as Doré's forest, and the menace implicit in the shiny, cold anonymity of the car—a familiar modern symbol of male status and power—is perhaps more meaningful for a contemporary reader than the sight of the "wolf" himself. As in Doré's illustration, the viewer bears the burden of anticipating Perrault's tragic ending. However, Moon's black-and-white photo-journalistic treatment of this very familiar story capitalizes on the ever-increasing currency of the visual medium, rendering the text all but extraneous. It also reminds us how familiar we are with the story that these photographs tell, as a glance at today's newspapers or magazines will confirm.

Another visualization of this same scene is to be found in the work of Mireille Levert (b. 1956)—but here we encounter an artist who is unequivocally illustrating the tale for the child-reader. The picture (Figure 3, 1995) is not without hints of menace, in the sudden bend in the path, the stance (not to mention the salivation) of the wolf, even the fallen tree that represents an additional obstacle for the little girl. And like many artists before her, Levert cannot resist the temptation to exploit the similarity between a tree root and an animal's claw! Yet these sinister aspects of the scene are mitigated by what we might term the cheerful plumpness of Levert's style, manifested in those same trees, which are somewhat reminiscent of ice-cream cones. As for the wolf, his back may be up, but the suggestion is of playfulness—true to pattern, the rocks look like tennis balls—rather than anger, even though readers young or old know that mischief is afoot. Most of all, the picture's roundness is concentrated in Little Red Riding Hood herself: she is virtually a series of circles, from nose to basket.

HANSEL AND GRETEL

Arthur Rackham (1867-1939) was one of the most eminent artists to emerge from what has become known as the Golden Age of children's book illustration (1860-1930). Rackham's wide and lasting popularity rests largely upon the appeal of his extraordinary fantasy worlds—believable because they are firmly rooted in reality. His attention to detail means that the witch and the stone step she stands upon are realistically depicted and thereby believable. In this sense, Rackham anticipates, in visual terms, J.R.R. Tolkien's creation of a believable "secondary world." Rackham's approach is evident in his illustration from "Hansel and Gretel" (front cover, 1903), in which the encounter between the children and the witch reveals a Dickensian combination of the realistic and the grotesque. Although Rackham's focus is clearly on the *human* drama, the observer is equally drawn in by the picturesque setting: the soothing quality of the sepia tones and the intricate delicacy of the details of wood, leaf, and stone. The attraction of the cottage is certainly not in the sweetness of its candy composition (which Rackham all but ignores) as in its romantic quaintness. We, like the children with whom we identify, long to see what lies beyond the antique bottle panes of the open window—surely a kettle on the boil and cookies in a jar—a welcoming home were it not for the witch who stands at the door. Illustrated is a moment of confrontation with the unexpected and forbidding on the one hand, and the welcoming and comforting, on the other, which Rackham reveals in the reactions and body postures of both witch and children. So potent is Rackham's mix of fantasy and reality that it imbues his world with an energy that promises a positive outcome to the confrontation.

The visualization by Kay Nielsen (1886-1957), of almost the same moment in the story, produces a very different picture. Nielsen's popularity rests largely upon his distinctive Art Deco style—although one may pause to wonder if its appeal is greater for the adult than the child. His illustration (Figure 4, 1925) for "Hansel and Gretel" is a case in point: the scene is infused with a nightmarish glamor as the surreal cottage crouches like a fluorescent spider in the middle of a web composed of sinuous, oppressive trees. The children are reduced to observers, sharing with us their fascination with the otherworldly oasis of color and light that lies before them. Despite—or is it because of?—the highly stylized approach, Nielsen's view draws us effectively into the story: the un-individualized children are here cast as our representatives—we too are waiting for that door to open ...

Like Sarah Moon in her version of "Little Red Riding Hood" (Figure 2), Anthony Browne (b. 1946) takes the step of giving "Hansel and Gretel" a modern setting: this family lives in a brick house containing many of the household items that populate our world also. Both artists, however, have been careful to evoke a contemporary setting that is nevertheless distant enough (vaguely mid-twentieth century) not to be exactly identifiable, thereby combining the open-endedness of "once upon a time" with the here-and-now. In Browne's opening illustration of the parlor (Figure 5, 1981), the familiar look of modern poverty is immediately apparent in the dirty, peeling wallpaper, the threadbare rug, and in the father's face and demeanor as he looks in vain through what is clearly the "Employment" section of the newspaper. More arresting, however, is the manner in which Browne manages to underline the crucial aspect of family dynamics and the stepmother's role in the lives of her husband and children. Browne sets her apart from the rest of her family: glamorous and comfortable, she watches a passenger jet take off on television. Through the symbols that permeate the picture—the abandoned "Gretel" doll, the bird mark on the ceiling—Browne paints us a story as meaningful as the words themselves. Illustrators such as Browne and Moon remind us that fairy tales, like Shakespeare's dramas, are as pertinent today as they ever were.

It takes no more than a glance at the work of Tony Ross (b. 1938) to realize that his approach (Figure 6, 1989) is quite different from that of the artists we have examined thus far: the contemporary cartoon style, the bright poster colors, the zany characterization all add to the slapstick mood that substantially reinvents the tale. Not surprisingly, Ross also re-writes the text, since it's clear that his irreverent style of illustration is incompatible with the serious tone of the Grimms' narrative. Both of the previous illustrations of this tale are strikingly static; we are invited to savor (or absorb) the moment. In this case, however, the moment is fleeting, since the action in Ross's picture is little short of manic; the witch is clearly no stranger to the concept of fast food. In keeping with this frenetic pace, the jokes come thick and fast; the *un*happy face on the mug, the tadpole jelly, the animal entourage ready and willing to partake of the feast—all contribute to the atmosphere of heedless self-gratification. If Browne's picture conveys a mood of gloomy withdrawal, here there is noise and bonhomie, as the witch takes wicked pleasure in exploiting the tendency of innocent children to have eyes bigger than their stomachs. Ross's approach may lack the historical detail or psychological complexity that dignifies other artists' approach to these tales, but his sense of the absurd provides clear evidence of the fairy tale's endless adaptability.

We have noted above that the style of Kay Nielsen's illustration owes much to Art Deco influences; likewise, we can detect unmistakable evidence of the Japanese *manga* comic style in the graphic-novel artwork (Figure 7, 2008) of Sean Dietrich (b. 1977). While the innocence and the anxious state of the children may provide psychological justification, the exaggerated eye-size (not to mention the unexpected hair color) has more to do with imposing familiar characteristics of a particular illustrative style on the world of the fairy tale. (We may detect a certain urban influence at work here, comparable to the environment in Anthony Browne's work.) This excerpt from *Hansel and Gretel* demonstrates how readily the tale can be adapted to the comic-book format: the simple morality, the flatness of character, and the emphasis upon sensational incident supply the graphic artist/writer with features remarkably similar to those of the comic book.

This reincarnation of the fairy tale in graphic novel format reveals that its evolution is as much circular as it is linear. Whatever its status among the guardians of culture and education over the centuries, the fairy tale has remained a staple of popular culture. Ignoring the scruples of its critics and any concern for quality, the purveyors of cheap broadsheets and chapbooks of the eighteenth century nevertheless satisfied the appetite for the fairy tale among the common people, many of whom would have been barely literate. Today's lavishly illustrated gift books notwithstanding, the fairy tale's resurgence in the "alternative" medium of the comic book provides ample evidence to support the view that through its versatility, its adaptability, and its universality, the tale is as healthy—and as relevant—today as it was a thousand years ago.

Nowhere is the role of the visual artist more obvious than in the popular medium of film, synonymous in the world of fairy tale with the work of Walt Disney. Indeed, our familiarity with fairy tales today is attributable almost exclusively to more than half a century of Disney's animated productions.

The transfer from book to screen represents an important qualitative leap in the recipient's experience of the tale. Quality and quantity of the illustrations notwithstanding, the book still provides the reader (or listener) with the text of the story and, thus, imaginative ownership of the material. The reader still has some ability to decide how much of an influence the visual images will have on his or her experience of the narrative. Nevertheless, the number, if not the quality, of pictures is bound to make a difference and, as we have seen, the growing tendency to illustrate fairy tales ever more profusely can have the effect of relegating the text to secondary importance. This predominance of the visual image at the expense of the text is, however, made complete in the medium of film. The most obvious contrast, of course, is the *complete* reliance on the visual image to re-create the story; without any text, each and every detail must be graphically represented—and many more details have to be invented, since the fairy tale leaves much to the imagination.

Not least is the problem of how to make the inherently dark side of fairy tales—their violence and cruelty—visually acceptable to a child audience. In *Snow White* (1937), his first animated tale, Disney had to deal with the stepmother's cannibalism, her three attempts to kill Snow White, and her subsequent horrific death. (Such a gruesome "happy ending" is not untypical of the fairy tale. Much of our satisfaction, in fact, derives from the inexorable working-out of poetic justice in the tales, however harsh it may be.) As with many illustrators confronted with the same issue, Disney's solution was to reduce or eliminate as much of the violent and cruel material as possible. However, the diminution of the stepmother's role and the two-dimensional doll-like portrayal of the characters, the comic characterization of the dwarves, the addition of domestic scenes with cute animal helpers, and the romantic ending—all to the accompaniment of cheerful song and dance—provide a radical departure from the spirit and essence of the original fairy tale. While Disney was quick to recognize and exploit the visually exciting potential of "scary" scenes which he added to the stories—one of the most memorable scenes from *Sleeping Beauty* (1959) is the battle between the Prince and Maleficent during which she transforms herself into a fire-breathing dragon—the effect was to replace the disturbing or

Figure 1: In the woods Little Red Riding Hood met old Father Wolf,
Les contes de Perrault, dessins par Gustav Doré (1867)

Figure 2: *Little Red Riding Hood* (1983), Sarah Moon

Figure 3: *Little Red Riding Hood* (1996), Mireille Levert

Figure 4: *Hansel and Gretel* (1925), Kay Nielsen

Figure 5: *Hansel and Gretel* (1981), Anthony Browne

Figure 6: *Hansel and Gretel* (1989), Tony Ross

Figure 7: *Hansel and Gretel: The Graphic Novel* (2008), Sean Dietrich

complex elements of the tale with the titillation of violence as spectacle—something Hollywood has always excelled at.

As his many critics have pointed out, Disney's shortcomings have less to do with his alteration of the story—the prerogative of every artist—than with his departure from the *spirit* of the fairy tale. As we pointed out at the beginning of this section, in re-working the raw material, the artist's response must be sensitive to its depth of meaning. In the process of translating these stories from book to screen, Disney reduced them to the romantic stereotypes and clichés that have given fairy tales a bad name, especially among feminist critics. Be that as it may, the enormous popularity of his productions makes a statement, which surely reveals more about our own attitudes and aspirations than about fairy tale. In this respect, it can be argued that Walt Disney was as much a man of his time as were the Brothers Grimm and Charles Perrault before him; they too manipulated the fairy tale to suit the tastes and expectations of their audience.

CRITICISM

SERIOUS CRITICAL ATTENTION TO THE fairy tale is essentially a phenomenon of the twentieth century. As we have noted in our introduction, discussion
prior to that tended to be dismissive, even condemnatory, despite the positive testi-
monials of various literary figures. In the English-speaking world, a breakthrough of
sorts came through the intervention of the eminent scholar and writer Andrew Lang
(1844-1912) who, through the publication of his twelve-volume "color" series, was
responsible for popularizing the fairy tale well beyond what we might term the classical canon of Perrault and the Grimms. As a folklorist, Lang was a representative of
a new field of study that seized upon the folk tale as a repository of valuable information about traditional beliefs, superstitions, and customs. This field of knowledge
was gradually absorbed into the larger discipline of anthropology, culminating in the
monumental project, initiated in Finland by Antti Aarne (1867-1925) and later taken
on by the American Stith Thompson (1885-1976), to produce a comprehensive index
of types and motifs to be found in the entire *corpus* of fairy tale.

Since these early years, the critical examination of the fairy tale has proceeded
apace, especially in the second half of the last century, and from a variety of different perspectives, the most notable being structuralist, psychological, and feminist.
Given the unique history and evolution of the fairy tale, however, problems can arise
if it is subjected to literary criteria that take no account of such matters as multiple
national and international variants and inadequate chronological evidence. From a
folkloristic perspective, this is, of course, a flawed methodology.

There can be little doubt that the most vigorous field of fairy-tale criticism over
the last forty years has been the feminist. Debate began with the publication in
1970 of "Fairy Tale Liberation,"[1] an essay by Alison Lurie, which in turn provoked

---

1   Lurie, Alison. "Fairy Tale Liberation." *The New York Review of Books*, December 17, 1970.

a spirited response from Marcia K. Lieberman, "'Some Day My Prince will Come': Female Acculturation through the Fairy Tale."[1] In exploring the myriad ways in which the female has been taught to accept a subordinate personal and social role, these and other feminist scholars quickly identified the fairy tale in particular as fostering such views. As we have seen, the fairy tale established itself as children's literature in the patriarchal nineteenth century, so it should come as no surprise that many of the most popular tales just happened to reflect and endorse this gender imbalance.

One medium that has quite simply revolutionized the fairy tale in the modern world is film—and in that field, the name of Walt Disney has reigned supreme. In the constant ebb and flow of our cultural scene, the Disney product has proved remarkably resilient, although that may be due more to skilful marketing than fidelity to the fairy tale—there is no clearer instance of what Jack Zipes has called the "commodification" of the fairy tale. While in no way excusing Disney for the liberties he (or his team) has taken with his raw material, Betsy Hearne, in her article "Disney Revisited, Or, Jiminy Cricket, It's Musty Down Here!" (1997), is nevertheless concerned that we judge Disney's intervention in the light of what has previously happened in the evolution of the fairy tale. As we have already seen, research has shown conclusively that what such luminaries as Perrault and the Grimms passed on to posterity was sometimes quite different from what they received. Thus, to condemn Disney for his influence is analogous to shooting the messenger, says Hearne. He has been successful, at least in part, because he has given us—children and adults alike—what we want.

In recent years, the production of animated fairy tales has been transformed into a competitive and enormously profitable business. The technological refinement in the magic of animation has brought about an extraordinary expansion in its appeal. Fantasy rules—and the fairy tale has continued to adapt (or, more accurately, it has *been* adapted) to changing circumstances. All this has not occurred without consequences, however, as James Poniewozik points out in a perceptive article in *Time* magazine (May 10, 2007) anticipating the opening of *Shrek 3*. He makes the point that in our media-dominated world, these sophisticated and elaborate parodies now represent the first exposure that many children have to the world of fairy tale. It is as if amid all the shock and awe of special effects and technological wizardry, the voice (and the companionship) of the storyteller has been all but drowned out; the audience's imagination has been short-circuited by watching the impossible made not just possible but downright easy, with the result that we are in danger of losing our

---

1   Lieberman, Marcia K. "'Some Day My Prince Will Come': Female Acculturation through the Fairy Tale." *College English* 34 (1972).

capacity to wonder. Poniewozik finds some cause for optimism in the creative invention that occasionally asserts itself amid all the "riffing on our cartoon patrimony," but there's no denying the strength of the cash-flow current.

DISNEY REVISITED, OR, JIMINY CRICKET, IT'S MUSTY DOWN HERE![1]

Betsy Hearne

I call him to account for his debasement of the traditional literature of childhood, in films and in the books he publishes:
He shows scant respect for the integrity of the original creations of authors, manipulating and vulgarizing everything for his own ends.
His treatment of folklore is without regard for its anthropological, spiritual, or psychological truths. Every story is sacrificed to the "gimmick" ... of animation....
Not content with the films, he fixes these mutilated versions in books which are cut to a fraction of their original forms, illustrates them with garish pictures, in which every prince looks like a badly drawn portrait of Cary Grant, every princess a sex symbol.

GUESS WHO FRANCES CLARKE SAYERS was talking about in 1965? This letter she published in the Los Angeles *Times* was printed as part of a longer article in *The Horn Book* (December 1965), and Walt Disney survived her attack by only one year. He died December 15, 1966. Three decades later, the single subject that will ensure debate among glazed undergraduates and exhausted graduate students of children's literature is criticism of a Walt Disney production. I have learned to muffle my salvos lest Disney devotees drop the course completely, but even so, one fan was close to tears when she exclaimed, "Can't you leave the poor man alone? He's dead!" This particular class presented me with a parting shot of three plastic figurines from the Disney Studios' *Beauty and the Beast*—plus the paperback spin-off.

Do Sayers's assertions of 1965 need an update? She was a sharp critic, preceding by a decade and more the landmark commentary of scholarly theorists, from Kay Stone ("Things Walt Disney Never Told Us," 1975) to Jack Zipes ("Breaking the Disney Spell," 1993). Disney is continuously under attack by critics of both academia

---

1   From *Horn Book Magazine*, March/April 1997.

and the popular press for messing up revered literature—witness the recently skewered *Hunchback of Notre Dame*. And Disney films are more wildly popular than ever. Is this cultural schizophrenia? The pro-Disney crowds at theaters and video stores speak in cash. The anti-Disney crowds speak in print. What's happening here? And what could anyone add, besides micro-analytic details, to Sayers's articulate assessment of the structural, tonal, stylistic, and didactic alterations with which Disney and company have "revised" traditional and/or classical stories?

Perhaps we can add just a bit of perspective. Disney's films changed within the forty-three years between his first Hollywood partnership with brother Roy in 1923, the year they released a short cartoon called *Alice's Wonderland*, and his last hands-on production, *The Jungle Book*, in 1966 (released posthumously in 1967). Disney films have changed between 1966 and 1996, too, and throughout both periods, the socio-economic and aesthetic context for Disney films has been changed by almost a century of events. To the audiences of the 1920s, Disney was entertainment. To the audiences of the 1960s, Disney was an icon. To the audiences of the 1990s, Disney is myth. In the absence of a permanent electrical blackout, the Disney Olympus is centrally mapped as a pinnacle in the kingdom of childhood. With just these few words, an image may have sprung to mind of the glowing castle with myriad spires thrusting phallically toward the heavens and triangulated banners waving over all.

Well, now that we're here, let's look over the landscape. Obviously, the concept of fairy-tale revision wasn't born with Disney in Chicago, Illinois, on December 5, 1901 (the same year *Peter Rabbit* was published, speaking of landmarks). In 1697 Charles Perrault refined some lusty old tales passed on by his children's nanny. In 1812 Wilhelm and Jacob Grimm made a real hit with the stories they collected from folk and family (more family than folk, as it turns out) and then revised, sometimes radically, over the next several editions of *Kinder- und Hausmärchen*. From 1889 to 1910 Andrew Lang stamped folk and fairy tales with his own style to the tune of ringing commercial success in a twelve-volume series starting with the *Blue Fairy Book* and proceeding through Red, Green, Yellow, Violet, and all the way to Lilac (multi-color literature was only a few letters short of multi-cultural, but the time wasn't ripe yet). Perrault, the Grimms, and Lang all addressed adults as much or more than children: Perrault and Lang with a wink-wink-nod-nod, and the Grimms with an agenda of glorifying—according to their lights—a cultural heritage. Is Disney the missing twentieth-century link in a chain of clever men who borrowed stories (often from anonymous women) and broadcast them via the latest mass medium? Whatever his critics say, Disney is even more of a cultural fact now than when he was alive. Thirty years worth of successful films produced by the studio that bears his name have extended his lifetime work beyond a mortal frame.

Now, of course, Perrault, Grimm, and Lang are, if not household words, at least uncontested cultural touchstones. And yet, in earlier chapters of high culture versus popular culture, they too had their share of detractors. It may come as no surprise that the folklore we so venerate today was once viewed as common and vulgar by the educated elite of the eighteenth and nineteenth centuries (most notably the moralistic Sarah Trimmer and Mrs. Sherwood). Will the newly created field of "Disney Studies" legitimize animated versions during the last quarter of the twentieth century in the same way that "Folklore Studies" legitimized printed versions in the last quarter of the nineteenth century? Are the changes "frozen" into film from the print tradition any more deleterious than the changes "frozen" into print from the oral tradition?

Sayers's attitude was that "folklore is a universal form, a great symbolic literature which represents the folk. It is something that came from the masses, not something that is put over on the masses.... Disney is basically interested in the market." Now, the market part is certainly still true. The Disney home videos I bought to review for this article included a snowfall of glossy pamphlets advertising The Cinderella Vacation Package, Tropicana orange juice and Pillsbury products and Cheerios (there must be a connection), and, of course, lots of Disney products in print, CD-ROM, and video format: "Play with Pocahontas, Sing-Along with Pooh, Roar with Simba, and Soar with Aladdin." Favorite films are released for only a few months on the home video market and then held off the market for several years ("Sleeping Beauty is in moratorium," announced the video salesman solemnly), just to ensure ongoing consumer appetite; it's a long-term strategy that works well to create a rush on any newly released golden oldie that won't be around long. This is not to mention the myriad toy, clothing, and other products that sell because of Disney characters' copyrighted graphic motifs. Of course, in a marketplace society any product has to make money—remember that the nineteenth-century folklorist Andrew Lang was not immune to the profits from his best-selling fairy-tale series—but the sheer sophistication and international dominance of the Disney commercial machine guarantee that a Disney version of a fairy tale or classic will be THE authorized version for millions and millions of young viewers all over the world. Do we criticize Disney simply because he is so successful in shaping so many children's imaginations into one mold? In that case, shouldn't we be criticizing the capitalist/mass media system itself (the cause) rather than its cultural freight trains (the symptom)?

Probably. But in any effort to countermand the Disneyfication of storylore, dissenting parents, teachers, and librarians are often frustrated by the film company's monolithic global influence. How many children (and adults) can we reach with alternative fairy-tale variants or with classics whose originals become sausage in Disney's grinder? As he said to one of his "story men" assigned to work on The Jungle

Book, "The first thing I want you to do is not to read it," adding later, "You can get all bogged down with these stories."

Remarks like this confirm every dissenter's objections to Disneyvision. Does this sound as curmudgeonly as Sayers's earlier remarks? Yes, but ... let's add some perspective to the rude facts, and here's where Sayers's assertions about the folk seem more questionable than her assertions about the films: "Folklore is a universal form, a great symbolic literature which represents the folk." Okay, but the folk keep changing; and although folklore is universal, the folk are not a universal unit. Further, she says of folklore: "It is something that came from the masses, not something that is put over on the masses"—as opposed to Disneylore, obviously, but that leads us to a conundrum. Disney *does* come from the masses as well as being put over on the masses, which we'll discuss further in a minute. Disney films represent the same chicken-and-egg syndrome as do the Barbie dolls his heroines so closely resemble. Our society exalts the impossible body form that Barbie represents, witness Playboy bunnies and Hollywood stars who have come closest to resembling her. Clearly, Mattel didn't originate that exalted body. But the dolls do perpetuate the exaltation through advertisement propaganda and mass distribution. Of course, there's also the little-studied question of what children do with those dolls. My kids cut off all their Barbies' hair and contorted the plastic bodies into what might benevolently be called positions of advanced yoga, but we'll try to stick to theory for a little longer and set aside the question of whether or not pernicious corporations are influencing every little girl to grow up wanting to look just like her Barbie doll (or a bald guru).

Although there's no question that private commerce manipulates public will, public will also shape private commerce, and both are shaped by social forces that influence the creation of and response to Disney's films. Dare we look at Disneylore as a grassroots movement, as electronic myth driven by social need as well as commercial greed, as formulae of exaggerated effects à la American tall tales? As even, perhaps, a form of parody, which his wry 1922 Laugh-o-Gram films of Little Red Riding Hood, Jack and the Beanstalk, Cinderella, and others so clearly were? Indeed, Disney's Hunchback of Notre Dame—based on a book that never, of course, was intended for children—takes parody to dizzying heights. Why is Jon Scieszka and Lane Smith's *The Stinky Cheese Man and Other Fairly Stupid Tales* or *The True Story of the Three Little Pigs*—along with a recent multitude of revisionist fairy tales—considered cleverly entertaining by so many children's book literati while Disney revisions, also cleverly entertaining, are deeply suspect? Why is it okay for feminists (of which I am one) to update passive heroines into active roles, or for socially sensitive library-storytellers (ditto) to omit elements of violence, racism, and other unacceptables from their story hours, and not for Disney to make changes, too? Do we really want to go graphic with heroes who trick their adversaries into eating a boiled relative, one of Brer Rabbit's escapades that somehow got left out of Disney's *Song of the South*? Can you just see animated blood dripping from the toes and shoes of Cinderella's sisters, per the Grimms' version, or two adorable little pigeons plucking out the sisters' eyes at Cinderella's wedding, one eye from each sister going into the church, and one eye from each sister coming back out? The folks at Disney want to make zippy productions and make everybody happy and make money, not hemorrhage all over the audience.

But also, you are qualified to ask, does every single story that Disney commandeers have to get so *cute* (except for the sensationally villainous scenes), no matter the tone of its ancestors? That charming little fellow we know as Jiminy Cricket, Pinocchio's conscience and commentator in Disney's film, was just an anonymous bug that got squashed in the beginning of Collodi's book. (Let me thank University of Illinois graduate student Bill Michtom for ranting and raving about this point.) Collodi's Pinocchio does bad stuff because he doesn't have a conscience; in Disney's version, he does bad stuff because of influence from villains. In other words, it's a lot easier to blame outer forces than inner forces, to see the evil in others rather than in ourselves or those with whom we identify. Is it the dark side, our own shadows, from which Disney protects the twentieth century? Are the children of today, who have never experienced a Depression or a World War, especially susceptible to a diet unbalanced toward the sprightly side with dancing teacups, singing seafood, twittering birds, and nose-twitching bunnies? Do there have to be quite so *many* animal helpers? That crowd of small mammals in *Snow White* seems on perpetual verge of stampede.

What are the real offenses Disney commits, aesthetically (distracting story gimmicks, hyperactive graphic images) and socially (violence, gender and ethnic stereotypes)? Certainly no one, not even Sayers, has objected to Disney originals such as Mickey Mouse, Donald Duck, *Lady and the Tramp*, and Roger Rabbit, for instance, or the various realistic nature/family dramas. What draws fire are the re-visions, the abandonment of past traditions for current values, which Disney reflects with unnerving accuracy. His first full-length feature, *Snow White and the Seven Dwarfs* (1937), embroidered basic fairy-tale formula with Hollywood romance, slapstick humor, and a Utopian alternative to the harsh competition engendered by the Depression (witness the cooperative work ethic of the seven miners and of the heroine's menagerie of housecleaners, an aspect that Terri Wright has explored in "Romancing the Tale: Walt Disney's Adaptation of the Grimms' 'Snow White'").

Some fifty years later, *Beauty and the Beast* has again emphasized romance and humor, but the Depression is long gone, and Disney films have long since entered the conservative mode adopted by Disney himself after World War II. Here we see cut-throat competition for Beauty's love in context of a violent society including a brutish suitor, a bloodthirsty mob, and a demonic insane-asylum director. While the household appliances are friendly, the Beast has acquired a vile temper, and even the animals have turned nasty, with a pack of wolves attacking Beauty, her father, and the Beast himself. The wolves' villainous role is particularly ironic because one of the earlier story's basic motifs was the transformational power of animal and human nature in balance.

Structurally, we've lost Beauty as hero: she who instigated the action by asking for a rose no longer asks for a rose; she who almost killed the Beast with her lack of perception but instead saved him by developing perception becomes an observer of two guys fighting over a girl. May the best man win. He does, but the woman has lost in the process. It's not enough to pay lip service to women's intelligence by propping a book up in front of a gorgeous female or showing her disdain for a macho suitor, when she's been denuded of her real power. Doesn't all this reflect an ongoing condition in our own society? Some of us don't like what we see here because we are seeing what's happening to us. Common television shows are full of it, but to watch a world-class artist like Disney glamorizing it is harder to take. On the other hand, in criticizing Disney, do we want to echo those who blame authors for producing books that reflect social problems we've created ourselves?

Without getting bogged down in a textual analysis based on scores of quotations from books and film scripts, we see over and over that Disney and company have given society not only what it will pay for, but also what it wants. The 1950 hit *Cinderella* spends as much time on Lucifer the cat chasing Gus and the other mice as it does on the main characters. Even Cinderella's return from the ball turns into a chase scene, not just the prince following her down a flight of stairs, but a wild pursuit of the king's horsemen thundering after her carriage. This device for escalating suspense is common to most of the animated features. Disney films have turned the folklore journey into a chase. What's added? Speed and competition, both key characteristics of our society. All you have to do is look at stories mythologized on television and you'll know how much our culture reverberates to chase scenes. Journeys of westward expansion turn into cowboy and Indian chase scenes; stories of crime and punishment turn into cops-and-robbers chase scenes. *Beauty and the Beast*, a television series that started with some tonal adherence to the main characters' slow-paced journeys of development, ended as a chase between Beast and the villain who stole his son (Beauty is murdered after giving birth). Disney's *Beauty and the Beast* is full of chase scenes instead of the journeys between castle and home that characterized Beauty's earlier journey of maturation.

The truth of it is that Disney's films relate less to their folkloric or literary predecessors than to their contemporary audience. While not all Disney's films have been equally popular, their reception does not depend on fidelity to any original. *Pinocchio*, *Peter Pan*, and *The Little Mermaid*, all of which veered wildly from Collodi's and Barrie's and Andersen's stories, were blockbusters. *Alice in Wonderland*, which veered wildly from Carroll's work, was a bust. The remake of *101 Dalmatians* stirred up some negative response not because it changed Dodie Smith's book, but because it changed the "original" film version! Success seems to depend on a film's fulfilling the Disney formula of visual and musical entertainment (a formula defined, circularly, by public response) and on fitting into the self-referential world established by the Disney canon.

This process begins with the very selection of the story itself. *The Little Mermaid* is the kind of persecuted female that Hans Christian Andersen loved to persecute even further (see also "The Red Shoes," "The Little Match Girl," etc.) and that Disney loved to rescue, sort of. Where are the swashbuckling heroines like Mollie Whuppie? Well, she's maybe a little too active, switching necklaces in the dark of night to trick her giant host into smashing the skulls of his own three daughters instead of Mollie and her sisters, whom he has planned to cook the next day. Tit for tat, you may say, but it would make a tough scene for the two-year-olds who swarm with their caretakers to the theater or sit propped before their electronic babysitters. A point here: the viewing crowd has gotten younger and younger over the century we're discussing, and the venues more intimate. What stranger can you trust in your children's bedroom but a film-maker whose sales figures depend on innocence and socially acceptable villainy? Murderous stepmothers seem to be okay; murderous fathers wouldn't be. Interesting, hunh? The Grimms, by the way, modulated their version of "Hansel and Gretel" through several editions to blame the children's abandonment first on the mother and father, then on the stepmother and father, then mostly on the stepmother.

Disney's modifications originate from accurate readings of our culture. He got the address right. This is where we live. We who criticize Disney have seen the enemy, and he is us. We are mistaken to speak as a voice removed from the rest of the population, as eighteenth- and nineteenth-century educators did in criticizing fairy tales and fiction, or to condemn artists as gulling the rest of the population. Disney belongs to us and we belong to him. What he does to fairy tales and classics is, in a sense, our own shadow. We don't have to like it and we don't have to keep quiet about it, but we do have to understand our own society and the lore it generates. The alternative is critical mustification. Popular culture and art are a vital dynamic. The past is always renegotiating with the present to become the future, and that requires the fresh air of our awareness.

"Beauty and the Beast" is a story I have loved all my life and studied for twenty years. Do I like what the Disney film has done to it? No, with qualifications. The scenes where the film-makers risk focusing on two characters' slowly maturing transformation—on the dance floor, for instance—are moving, and the animated art is rich. However, the violation of profound elements and the frenetic pace bother me in the film just as they bother me in everyday life. Does my opinion matter? Yes, but there are better ways to express it than boycotting the film or keeping it from my kids. They live here, too. They need to know what's going on, just as I do. We've watched and discussed it together; they cheer while I rant and rave. Disney is fun, they remind me. Our society craves fun, I remind them—but isn't there something else to life? Sure, Mom.

So, can we have fun and still challenge what's fun? Can we aim our criticism not at censuring/censoring an artistic reality, but at changing the self, family, and society that inspires and supports it? Sure we can, kids.

Obviously, all parents should follow their instincts about whether or not—and at what age—to expose their children to Disneyed stories. However, we may be mistaken to overestimate the changes Disney makes and underestimate the changes we can make. In one of my favorite anecdotes, from the ChildLit Listserv, Megan L. Isaac describes a four-year-old who after months of pleading was finally given Beauty and the Beast dolls that were then being promoted as merchandising tie-ins for the film. (Previously her parents had resisted purchasing a Barbie, so they were loath to give in to this similar model of female perfection.) Anyway, as the adults chatted, she sat on the floor blissfully playing with her two new dolls and creating a dialogue between them. A rough paraphrase follows:

> Beast: Come on, Beauty, you have to come live in my castle.
> Beauty: No, I don't want to.
> Beast: You have to. I say so.
> Beauty: No I don't. You're not my boss. I'm going to put you in the zoo.

Here's to the film-makers of the future!

THE END OF FAIRY TALES? HOW SHREK AND FRIENDS HAVE CHANGED CHILDREN'S STORIES[1]

James Poniewozik

ONCE UPON A TIME, IN a land near near by, there were fairy tales. Brave princes slew dragons and saved fair damsels. Princesses and scullery maids waited for brave knights and true love. The good were pretty, the evil ugly, the morals absolute. And lo, it was good. If you liked that sort of thing.

Then a hideous green monster appeared and threw the realm into chaos. Handsome princes were mocked, damsels saved themselves, and ogres and dragons were shown to be decent folks once you got to know them.

And lo, it was even better—particularly for the movie industry. The first two *Shrek* movies, which upended every fairy-tale cliché they could get their meaty chartreuse paws on, grossed more than $700 million in the U.S. alone; there's little reason to believe that *Shrek the Third* won't fill its hungry Scottish maw with hundreds of millions more after it is released May 18 [2007].

Shrek consciously rebelled against the sentimental Disney hegemony of fairy-tale movies. But today the outlaw is king: parodying fairy tales has become the default mode of telling them. 2005's *Hoodwinked!* reimagined *Little Red Riding Hood* as a crime *Rashomon*, while this year's *Happily N'Ever After* sent up *Cinderella*. Broadway smash *Wicked* posits that the Wicked Witch of the West was misunderstood. This fall Disney (*et tu*, Mickey?) releases *Enchanted*, in which a princess (Amy Adams) is magically banished by an evil queen to modern New York City, where she must fend for herself, parodying her princess foremothers as she goes. (*Snow White's Whistle While You Work* scene is re-enacted with vermin and roaches.)

All this has been a welcome change from generations of hokey fairy tales with stultifying lessons: Be nice and wait for your prince; be obedient and don't stray off the path; bad people are just plain evil and ugly and deserve no mercy. But palace revolutions can have their own excesses. Are the rules of fairy-tale snark becoming as rigid as the ones they overthrew? Are we losing a sense of wonder along with all the illusions?

Shrek didn't remake fairy tales single-handed; it captured, and monetized, a long-simmering cultural trend. TV's *Fractured Fairy Tales* parodied Grimm classics, as have movies like *The Princess Bride* and *Ever After* and the books on which *Shrek* and *Wicked* were based. And highbrow postmodern and feminist writers, such as Donald Barthelme and Angela Carter, Robert Coover and Margaret Atwood, used the raw material of fairy stories to subvert traditions of storytelling that were as ingrained in

---

1   From *Time Magazine*, 10 May 2007.

us as breathing or to critique social messages that their readers had been fed along with their strained peas.

But those parodies had a dominant fairy-tale tradition to rebel against. The strange side effect of today's meta-stories is that kids get exposed to the parodies before, or instead of, the originals. My two sons (ages 2 and 5) love *The Three Pigs*, a storybook by David Wiesner in which the pigs escape the big bad wolf by physically fleeing their story (they fold a page into a paper airplane to fly off in). It's a gorgeous, fanciful book. It's also a kind of recursive meta-fiction that I didn't encounter before reading John Barth in college. Someday the kids will read the original tale and wonder why the stupid straw-house pig doesn't just hop onto the next bookshelf. Likewise, *Shrek* reimagines Puss in Boots as a Latin tomcat—but what kid today even reads *Puss in Boots* in the original?

This is the new world of fairy tales: parodied, ironized, meta fictionalized, politically adjusted and pop culture saturated. (Yes, the original stories are still out there, but they don't have the same marketing force behind them: the Happy Meals, action figures, books, games and other ancillary revenue projects.) All of which appeals to the grownups who chaperone the movie trips and endure the repeated DVD viewings. Old school fairy tales, after all, are boring to us, not the kids. The *Shrek* movies have a nigh scientific formula for the ratio of fart jokes to ask your mother jokes; *Shrek the Third* includes a visit to a fairy tale high school where there's a Just Say Nay rally and a stoner sounding kid stumbles out of a coach trailed by a cloud of "frankincense and myrrh" smoke. More broadly, each movie gives Shrek and Fiona an adult challenge: in the first, to find love and see beyond appearances; in *Shrek 2*, to meet the in-laws; in *Shrek the Third*, to take on adult responsibility and parenthood (Shrek has to find a new heir to the throne of Far Far Away, or he will have to succeed the king).

Then there are the messages aimed at kids. What parent today wants to raise an entitled prince or a helpless damsel? Seeing Snow White turn from cream puff into kick-ass fury in *Shrek the Third*—launching an army of bluebirds and bunnies at the bad guys to the tune of Led Zeppelin's *Immigrant Song*—is more than a brilliant sight gag. It's a relief to parents of girls, with Disney's princess legacy in their rearview mirrors and Bratz dolls and Britney up ahead. It goes hand in hand with a vast genre of empowered-princess books (*Princess Smartypants*, *The Princess Knight*) for parents who'd rather their daughters dream of soccer balls than royal balls. As for the boys? Jocks have a rough time of it (a handsome prince is the villain of *Shrek the Third* and the buffoon in *N'Ever After*), supplanted by gangly emo types—fairyland Adam Brodys. "Charming" is redefined rather than repealed—Justin Timberlake voices *Third's* cute-boy hero Arthur—but at least that's some progress.

Tweaking fairy tales also allows moviemakers to tell stories about themselves without boring us. The *Shrek* movies are full of inside jokes (the kingdom of Far Far Away is essentially Beverly Hills; the first villain was widely seen as a stand-in for then Disney chief Michael Eisner). Fairy-tale parodies are safe rebellions, spoofing formulas and feel-good endings while still providing the ride into the sunset that pays the bills. In *Happily N'Ever After*, a wizard runs a "Department of Fairy-tale-land Security," seeing to it that each story—*Rapunzel, Rumpelstiltskin*, etc.—hews to the book. His bored apprentice Mambo articulates the strategy of his movie and its peers: "I just wish we could mix it up a little. Make it a little edgier! Then let 'em have their happy ending."

Sound like a formula to you? What these stories are reacting against is not so much fairy tales in general as the specific, saccharine Disney kind, which sanitized the far-darker originals. (As did *Shrek*, by the way. In the William Steig book, the ogre is way more brutal, scary and ... ogreish.) But the puncturing of the Disney style is in danger of becoming a cliché itself. The pattern—set up, then puncture, set up, then puncture—is so relentless that it inoculates the audience against being spellbound, training them to wait for the other shoe to drop whenever they see a moment of sentiment or magic. Every detail argues against seeing fairyland as something special, like the constant disposable-culture gags in *Shrek*, in which characters shop in chain stores like Versarchery and Ye Olde Foot Locker.

I feel like a traitor to my fellow parents for even saying this. These movies are made in part for me: a socially progressive, irony-friendly Gen Xer with rug rats. I thought *Hoodwinked!* and most of the *Shrek* series were hilarious, and God knows I don't want to go back to the days of suffering with my kids through a long, slow pour of Uncle Walt's wholesome syrup. But even if you ultimately reject their messages, old-school fairy tales are part of our cultural vocabulary. There's something a little sad about kids growing up in a culture where their fairy tales come pre-satirized, the skepticism, critique and revision having been done for them by the mama birds of Hollywood. Isn't irony supposed to derive from having something to rebel against? Isn't there a value in learning, for yourself, that life doesn't play out as simply as it does in fairy tales? Is there room for an original, nonparodic fairy story that's earnest without being cloying, that's enlightened without saying wonder is for suckers?

In fact, the strongest moments in *Shrek the Third* come when it steps back from the frantic pop-culture name dropping of *Shrek 2* and you realize that its Grimm parodies have become fleshed-out characters in their own right. In August [2007], Paramount releases *Stardust*, an adaptation of a Neil Gaiman novel about a nerdy nineteenth-century lad who ventures from England to a magical land to retrieve a fallen star. The live-action movie covers many of the same themes as the ubiquitous cartoon parodies—be yourself, don't trust appearances, women can be heroic too.

But it creates its own fantastic settings (a seedy witches' bazaar, a sky pirate's dirigible ship). There's a kind of surprise and unembarrassed majesty that come from minting original characters and imagery rather than simply riffing on our cartoon patrimony. In the end, that's how you make magic.

SELECTED BIBLIOGRAPHY

Critical/General

Ashliman, D.L. *Folk and Fairy Tales: A Handbook*. Westport, CT: Greenwood P, 2004.

Bacchilega, Cristina. *Postmodern Fairy Tales: Gender and Narrative Strategies*. Philadelphia: U of Pennsylvania P, 1997.

Baker, Donald. *Functions of Folk and Fairy Tales*. Washington, DC: Association for Childhood Education International, 1981.

Beckett, Sandra. *Recycling Red Riding Hood*. New York: Routledge, 2002.

Bottigheimer, Ruth B. *Fairy Tales: A New History*. Albany: State U of New York P, 2009.

_____, ed. *Fairy Tales and Society: Illusion, Allusion and Paradigm*. Philadelphia: U of Pennsylvania P, 1986.

Canepa, Nancy, ed. *Out of the Woods: The Origins of the Literary Fairy Tale in Italy and France*. Detroit: Wayne State UP, 1997.

Davidson, Hilda E. and Anna Chaudri, eds. *A Companion to the Fairy Tale*. Cambridge: D.S. Brewer, 2003.

De Vos, Gail and Anna E. Altmann. *New Tales for Old: Folktales as Literary Fictions for Young Adults*. Englewood, CO: Teacher Ideas P, 1999.

Dundes, Alan, ed. *Cinderella: A Casebook*. Madison: U of Wisconsin P, 1988.

_____. *Little Red Riding Hood: A Casebook*. Madison: U of Wisconsin P, 1989.

Houghton, Rosemary. *Tales from Eternity: The World of Fairy Tales and the Spiritual Search*. New York: Seabury P, 1973.

Jones, Steven Swann. *The Fairy Tale: The Magic Mirror of Imagination*. New York: Twayne, 1995.

Knoepflmacher, U.C. *Ventures into Childland: Victorians, Fairy Tales and Femininity*. Chicago: U of Chicago P, 1999.

Lane, Marcia. *Picturing the Rose: A Way of Looking at Fairy Tales*. New York: H.W. Wilson, 1994.

Lurie, Alison. *Don't Tell the Grown-ups: Subversive Children's Literature*. Boston: Little, Brown, 1990.

Lüthi, Max. *Once Upon a Time: On the Nature of Fairy Tales*. Trans. Lee Chadeayne and Paul Gottwald. New York: Frederick Ungar, 1970.

_____. *The European Folktale: Form and Nature*. Trans. John D. Niles. Bloomington: Indiana UP, 1982.

_____. *The Fairy Tale as Art Form and Portrait of Man*. Trans. Jon Erickson. Bloomington: Indiana UP, 1984.

McGlathery, James M. *Fairy Tale Romance: The Grimms, Basile and Perrault*. Urbana: U of Illinois P, 1991.

Orenstein, Catherine, *Little Red Riding Hood Uncloaked: Sex, Morality and the Evolution of a Fairy Tale.* New York: Basic Books, 2002.

Rohrich, Lutz. *Folktales and Reality.* Trans. Peter Tokofsky. Bloomington: Indiana UP, 1991.

Sale, Roger. *Fairy Tales and After: From Snow White to E.B. White.* Cambridge, MA: Harvard UP, 1978.

Schectman, Jacqueline M. *The Stepmother in Fairy Tales.* Boston: Sigo P, 1991.

Tatar, Maria M. *Off with Their Heads!: Fairy Tales and the Culture of Childhood.* Princeton, NJ: Princeton UP, 1992.

Thomas, Joyce. *Inside the Wolf's Belly: Aspects of the Fairy Tale.* Sheffield, UK: Sheffield Academic P, 1989.

Tolkien, J.R.R. *Tree and Leaf.* Boston: HoughtonMifflin, 1965.

Travers, P.L. *About the Sleeping Beauty.* New York: McGraw-Hill, 1975.

Warner, Marina. *From the Beast to the Blonde.* London: Chatto and Windus, 1994.

Yolen, Jane. *Touch Magic: Fantasy, Faerie and Folklore in the Literature of Childhood.* New York: Philomel, 1981.

Zipes, Jack D. *Breaking the Magic Spell: Radical Theories of Folk and Fairy Tales.* 2nd ed. Lexington: UP of Kentucky, 2002.

_____. *Fairy Tale as Myth : Myth as Fairy Tale.* Lexington: UP of Kentucky, 1994.

_____. *Fairy Tales and the Art of Subversion: The Classic Genre for Children and the Process of Civilization.* 2nd ed. New York: Routledge, 2006.

_____. *Happily Ever After: Fairy Tales, Children, and the Culture Industry.* New York: Routledge, 1997.

_____, ed. *The Trials and Tribulations of Little Red Riding Hood.* 2nd ed. New York: Routledge, 1993.

_____. *When Dreams Came True: Classical Fairy Tales and Their Tradition.* 2nd ed. New York: Routledge, 2007.

Brothers Grimm

Bottigheimer, Ruth B. *Grimms' Bad Girls and Bold Boys: The Moral and Social Vision of the Tales.* New Haven: Yale UP, 1987.

Ellis, John M. *One Fairy Story Too Many: The Brothers Grimm and Their Tales.* Chicago: U of Chicago P, 1983.

Haase, Donald, ed. *The Reception of Grimms' Fairy Tales: Responses, Reactions, Revisions.* Detroit: Wayne State UP, 1993.

Kamenetsky, Christa. *The Brothers Grimm and Their Critics: Folk Tales and the Quest for Meaning.* Athens: Ohio UP, 1992.

Kudszus, Winfried. *Terrors of Childhood in Grimms' Fairy Tales.* New York: P. Lang, 2005.

McGlathery, James M., ed. *The Brothers Grimm and Folk Tale.* Urbana: U of Illinois P, 1988.

_____. *Grimms' Fairy Tales: A History of Criticism on a Popular Classic.* Columbia, SC: Camden House, 1993.

Michaelis-Jena, Ruth. *The Brothers Grimm.* New York: Praeger, 1970.

Murphy, G. Ronald. *The Owl, the Raven and the Dove: The Religious Meaning of the Grimms' Magic Fairy Tales.* Oxford: Oxford UP, 2000.

Peppard, Murray. *Paths Through the Forest: A Biography of the Brothers Grimm.* New York: Holt, Rinehart & Winston, 1971.

Tatar, Maria. *The Hard Facts of the Grimms' Fairy Tales.* Revised ed. Princeton, NJ: Princeton UP, 2003.

Zipes, Jack. *The Brothers Grimm: From Enchanted Forests to the Modern World.* 2nd ed. New York: Palgrave Macmillan, 2003.

Perrault and the French

Barchilon, Jacques and Peter Flinders. *Charles Perrault*. Boston: Twayne Publishers, 1981.

Darnton, Robert. *The Great Cat Massacre and Other Episodes in French Cultural History*. New York: Basic Books, 1984.

Hearne, Betsy G. *Beauty and the Beast: Visions and Revisions of an Old Tale*. Chicago: U of Chicago P, 1989.

Lewis, Philip. *Seeing Through the Mother Goose Tales: Visual Turns in the Writings of Perrault*. Stanford: Stanford UP, 1996.

Morgan, Jeanne. *Perrault's Morals for Moderns*. New York: Peter Lang, 1985.

Seifert, Lewis. *Fairy Tales, Sexuality and Gender in France, 1690-1715: Nostalgic Utopias*. New York: Cambridge UP, 1996.

Tatar, Maria. *Secrets beyond the Door: The Story of Bluebeard and His Wives*. Princeton NJ: Princeton UP, 2006.

Andersen

Bredsdorff, Elias. *Hans Christian Andersen*. New York: Charles Scribner's Sons, 1975.

Gronbech, Bo. *Hans Christian Andersen*. Boston: Twayne Publishers, 1980.

Lederer, Wolfgang. *The Kiss of the Snow Queen: Hans Christian Andersen and Man's Redemption by Woman*. Berkeley: U of California P, 1986.

Spink, Reginald. *Hans Christian Andersen and His World*. New York: G.P. Putnam's Sons, 1972.

Zipes, Jack. *Hans Christian Andersen: The Misunderstood Storyteller*. New York: Routledge, 2005.

Psychological

Bettelheim, Bruno. *The Uses of Enchantment: The Meaning and Importance of Fairy Tales*. New York: Alfred Knopf, 1976.

Bly, Robert. *Iron John: A Book about Men*. New York: Vintage, 1992.

Cashdan, Sheldon. *The Witch Must Die: How Fairy Tales Shape Our Lives*. New York: HarperCollins, 2000.

Chinen, Allan B. *In the Ever After: Fairy Tales and the Second Half of Life*. Wilmette, IL: Chiron Publications, 1989.

_____. *Once Upon a Midlife: Classical Stories and Mythic Tales to Illuminate the Middle Years*. Los Angeles: Jeremy Tarcher, 1992.

Dieckmann, Hans. *Twice-Told Tales: The Psychological Use of Fairy Tales*. Wilmette, IL: Chiron, 1986.

Franz, Marie Louise von. *An Introduction to the Psychology of Fairy Tales*. 3rd ed. Zurich: Spring Publications, 1975.

_____. *Individuation in Fairy Tales*. Zurich: Spring Publications, 1977.

_____. *Problems of the Feminine in Fairy Tales*. Irving, TX: Spring Publications, 1979.

Fromm, Erich. *The Forgotten Language: An Introduction to the Understanding of Dreams, Fairy Tales and Myths*. New York: Grove P, 1951.

Heuscher, Julius. *A Psychiatric Study of Myths and Fairy Tales: Their Origin, Meaning and Usefulness*. Springfield, IL: Thomas, 1974.

Livo, Norma. *Who's Afraid ... ? Facing Children's Fears with Folktales.* Englewood, CO: Teacher Ideas P, 1994.

Mallet, Carl-Heinz. *Fairy Tales and Children: The Psychology of Children Revealed Through Four of Grimms' Fairy Tales.* New York: Schocken Books, 1984.

Metzger, Michael and Katherina Mommsen, eds. *Fairy Tales as Ways of Knowing: Essays on Märchen in Psychology, Society and Literature.* Bern: P. Lang, 1981.

Anthropological/Folkloric/Linguistic

Aarne, Antti, and Stith Thompson. *The Types of the Folktale: A Classification and Bibliography.* Helsinki: FF Communications 184, 1961.

Degh, Linda. *Folktales and Society: Storytelling in a Hungarian Peasant Community.* Trans. Emily M. Schossberger. Bloomington: Indiana UP, 1969.

_____. *Folklore and the Mass Media.* Bloomington: Indiana UP, 1994.

Dundes, Allan, ed. *Analytic Essays in Folklore.* The Hague: Mouton, 1975.

_____. *The Study of Folklore.* Englewood Cliffs, NJ: Prentice-Hall, 1965.

Dorson, Richard. *Folklore.* Bloomington: Indiana UP, 1972.

Hartland, E.S. *The Science of Fairy Tales: An Enquiry into Fairy Mythology.* Detroit: Singing Tree P, 1968.

Propp, Vladimir. *The Morphology of the Folktale.* Austin: U of Texas P, 1968.

Thompson, Stith. *The Folktale.* New York: Holt, Reinhart and Winston, 1946.

Yearsley, Percival M. *The Folklore of Fairy Tale.* Detroit: Singing Tree P, 1968.

Feminist

Estes, Clarissa Pinkola. *Women Who Run with the Wolves: Myths and Stories of the Wild Woman Archetype.* New York: Ballantyne, 1992.

Farrer, Claire, ed. *Women and Folklore.* Austin: U of Texas P, 1975.

Gould, Joan. *Spinning Straw into Gold: What Fairy Tales Reveal about the Transformations in a Woman's Life.* New York: Random House, 2006.

Haase, Donald, ed. *Fairy Tales and Feminism: New Approaches.* Detroit: Wayne State UP, 2004.

Harries, Elizabeth Wanning. *Twice Upon a Time: Women Writers and the History of the Fairy Tale.* Princeton, NJ: Princeton UP, 2001.

Kolbenschlag, Madonna. *Kiss Sleeping Beauty Goodbye.* Garden City, NY: Doubleday, 1979.

Rusch-Feja, Diann. *The Portrayal of the Maturation Process in Girl Figures in Selected Tales of the Brothers Grimm.* Frankfurt-am-Mein: Peter Lang, 1995.

Walker, Barbara. *Feminist Fairy Tales.* New York: HarperCollins, 1997.

Zipes, Jack D., comp. *Don't Bet on the Prince: Contemporary Feminist Fairy Tales in North America and England.* New York: Methuen, 1986.

Illustration and Film

Bell, Elizabeth, Lynda Haas, and Laura Sells, eds. *From Mouse to Mermaid: The Politics of Film, Gender, and Culture.* Bloomington: Indiana UP, 1995.
Holliss, Richard and Brian Sibley. *Walt Disney's* Snow White and the Seven Dwarfs *and the Making of the Classic Film.* New York: Simon & Schuster, 1987.
Meyer, Susan E. *A Treasury of the Great Children's Book Illustrators.* New York: Harry Abrams, 1987.
Nodelman, Perry. *Words about Pictures: The Narrative Art of Children's Picture Books.* Athens: U of Georgia P, 1988.
Schickel, Richard. *The Disney Version: The Life, Times, Art and Commerce of Walt Disney.* New York: Simon Schuster, 1985.

Journals

Below are listed the major journals in which numerous articles on folk and fairy tales may found.

Canadian Children's Literature (CanCL)
Children's Literature (CL)
Children's Literature Association Quarterly (ChLAQ)
Children's Literature in Education (CLE)
Horn Book
The Lion and the Unicorn (LU)
Signal

Websites

Three websites that provide a wealth of tales and reference materials

<http://www.pitt.edu/~dash/folklinks.html>
<http://www.pitt.edu/~dash/folktexts.html>
<http://www.surlalunefairytales.com>

TEXTUAL SOURCES

Afanas'ev, Aleksandr
"Vasilisa the Beautiful," from *The Collections of Aleksandr Afanas'ev Russian Fairy Tales*. Translated by Norbery Guterman. 2nd edition. New York: Pantheon Books, 1945. Copyright © 1945 by Afanas'ev, Aleksandr. Used by permission of Pantheon Books, a division of Random House, Inc.

Andersen, Hans Christian
"The Ugly Duckling," from *Hans Christian Andersen: His Classic Fairy Tales*. Edited by Erik Hauggaard. Copyright © 1974 by Erik Christian Haugaard. Used by permission of Doubleday, a division of Random House, Inc.

Basile, Giambattista
"Sun, Moon, and Talia," from *The Pentamerone*. Translated by Benedetto Croce. Edited by N.M. Penzer. London: John Lane, The Bodley Head, 1932. Reprinted by permission of The Random House Group Ltd.

Block, Francesca Lia
"Wolf," from *The Rose and the Beast: Fairy Tales Retold*. New York: HarperCollins, 2000. Copyright © 2000 by Francesca Lia Block. Reprinted by permission of HarperCollins Publishers.

Bushnaq, Inea
"The Little Red Fish and the Clog of Gold," from *Arab Folktales*. New York: Pantheon Press, 1986. Copyright © 1986 by Inea Bushnaq. Used by permission of Alfred A. Knopf, a division of Random House, Inc.

McPhail, David
Little Red Riding Hood. New York: Scholastic, Inc., 1995. Copyright © 1995 by David McPhail. Reprinted by permission of Scholastic Inc.

Perrault, Charles
"Little Red Riding Hood," "The Sleeping Beauty in the Wood," "Cinderella," and "Hop o' my Thumb," from *Sleeping Beauty and Other Favorite Tales*. Translated by Angela Carter. New York: Penguin Classics, 2008. Copyright © 1992 by Angela Carter. Reprinted by permission of Penguin, A Member of Penguin Group (USA) Inc., 345 Hudson Street, New York, NY 10014. All rights reserved.

ILLUSTRATION SOURCES

Little Red Riding Hood and the Car by Sarah Moon. Copyright © 1983 Sarah Moon. Reproduced by permission of The Creative Company, Mankato, MN.

Little Red Riding Hood Meets the Wolf by Mireille Levert from *Little Red Riding Hood*. Toronto: Groundwood Book, 1995. Copyright © 1995 by Mireille Levert. Reproduced by permission of Douglas & McIntyre Ltd.

Hansel and Gretel by Kay Neilsen from *Hansel and Gretel, and Other Stories by the Brothers Grimm*. Reproduced by permission of Hodder and Stoughton Limited.

Hansel and Gretel by Anthony Browne. Copyright © 1981, 2003 by Anthony Browne. Reproduced by permission of Walker Books, Ltd., London SE11 5HJ.

Illustration from *Hansel and Gretel* by Tony Ross. London: Andersen Press, 1989. Copyright © 1989 by Tony Ross. Reproduced by permission of Andersen Press.

Page 10 from *Hansel and Gretel: The Graphic Novel* illustrated by Sean Dietrich. Minneapolis: Stone Arch Books, 2008. Copyright © 2008 by Sean Dietrich.